ALSO BY KERRIE DROBAN

Vagos, Mongols, and Outlaws: My Infiltration of

America's Deadliest Bike Gangs (with Charles Falco)

Socialite Scorned: The Murder of a Tucson High-Roller

Prodigal Father, Pagan Son: Growing Up Inside the

Dangerous World of the Pagans Motorcycle Club

(with Anthony "LT" Menginie)

unning with the Devil: The True Story of the ATF's

Infiltration of the Hells Angels

The Last Chicago Boss

MY LIFE WITH THE CHICAGO OUTLAWS MOTORCYCLE CLUB

PETER "BIG PETE" JAMES

with KERRIE DROBAN

St. Martin's Press
New York

THE LAST CHICAGO BOSS. Copyright © 2017 by Peter "Big Pete" James with Kerrie Droban. All rights reserved. Printed in the United States of America. For information, address St. Martin's Press, 175 Fifth Avenue, New York, N.Y. 10010.

www.stmartins.com

Designed by Omar Chapa

The Library of Congress Cataloging-in-Publication Data
is available upon request.

ISBN 978-1-250-10591-2 (hardcover)
ISBN 978-1-250-18730-7 (ebook)

Our books may be purchased in bulk for promotional, educational, or business use. Please contact your local bookseller or the Macmillan Corporate and Premium Sales Department at 1-800-221-7945, extension 5442, or by email at MacmillanSpecialMarkets@macmillan.com.

First Edition: September 2017

10 9 8 7 6 5 4 3 2 1

For my wife, Debbie

CONTENTS

Preface .... *xi*

Dark Ride *1*

PART I

1. Born This Way 5
2. Let The Games Begin 19
3. My Playbook 29
4. The Loyal Order 45
5. On The Island Of Misfit Toys 54
6. Deconstructing Charlie 66
7. Wiseguys 78
8. Rock Star 87
9. We, The People 95
10. Neutral Ground 103
11. The Angels Are Coming 113
12. Run 123
13. Life Of The Party 128
14. The Other Me 136

15. Guns N' Roses 144

16. Lobster Sauce 149

17. Burning Down The House 158

18. Karate G-Man 173

19. God Forgives, Outlaws Don't 181

20. The Fall 189

PART II

21. Shelter From The Storm 213

22. Ho Jo 225

23. The Cosmic Riders 231

24. The Business Of Business 238

25. High Noon 246

26. The Help 257

27. Game Over 272

PS *281*

Acknowledgments *285*

AUTHOR'S NOTE

This is a true story, though some names and details have been changed.

PREFACE

Death ends a life, not a relationship.

—TUESDAYS WITH MORRIE

"I'm dying," Pete began our first conversation. He asked me to write his life story. "I am the last Chicago Boss of the Outlaws," one of the most ruthless motorcycle gangs in the world. We could not have been more different; yet, as we embarked on this yearlong odyssey, involving hundreds of hours of interviews, recordings, intimate disclosures, confidential insights into gang life, and scary revelations about the ever-thinning blue line between cop and criminal and criminal cop, we formed a fierce friendship full of poetry, confession, and heart.

But Pete "never wanted my heart, he wanted my soul."

He sent me classical compositions; his favorite, Chopin's "Spring Waltz," reminded him of rebirth and hope. Selections from Marshall Tucker and Bob Dylan conjured up abandon, open road, and the kind of lonely freedom reserved for *pure* outlaws.

"Smile, Kerrie Kerrie. I've lived a charmed life."

He insisted I "saved him" from spinning into dark oblivion and then declared, "This isn't *my* story, Kerrie Kerrie, it's *yours*."

And perhaps in a way it is the culmination of my life's work: the intense study of criminal pathology, dark subcultures, and the toxic cocktail that makes us all monstrously human. I am thankful, Pete—particularly in your world, where "women are more dangerous than shotguns"*—to have learned the most intimate parts of *your* soul.

---

* Calo, *The Godfather*

Pete riding down I-290 into Chicago (Sears Tower)

Life is a state of mind.

—PRESIDENT "BOBBY," *BEING THERE*

DARK RIDE

When a man is denied the right to live the life he believes in, he has no choice but to become an outlaw.

—NELSON MANDELA

My Harley hugged the curves on the Dan Ryan Expressway. Tires dipped into small grooves full of glass chips, stripped rubber, and crushed bits of rock. Gold lights flickered off Lake Michigan. I led a pack of twenty Chicago Outlaws. We shot through nightfall in tight formation like vampire bats.

Our patch, red-eyed "Charlie," the skull-and-cross pistons that defined the Outlaws Motorcycle Club (OMG), glared at hitchhikers, trucks, and cars with zipped-up windows. One spooked motorist slowed to ogle our spectacle and collided into a meat truck; its side door caved in, crumpled up like tinfoil. Chunks of ice flew out, cracking windshields. Frozen packaged animal heads littered the roadway. Sirens wailed in the distance.

I cracked the throttle wide open, pulling away from a potential pileup as car after car slammed brakes, honked horns, and swerved dangerously close to the guardrails.

A lone biker zigzagged the white line; he was a moving target, easy to pick off with a shot to the neck, or a pop to his tire. His life depended on his colors and the turf he claimed . . . and whether he was a Hells Angel.

The stranger sped up and tucked between two vans. His tire backfired, sounded like gunshot. A streetlamp burst. The rear van lurched and swerved and slammed his brakes, forcing the biker to veer sharply toward the exit ramp. His body sailed forward, skidding to a dusty halt like a stuntman rehearsing for an action film.

Perhaps we should have rendered aid, but we were Outlaws in running formation, moving like a black mass, in sleeveless leather vests, skullcaps, and skeleton half-face masks. And Bob Dylan's "Man of Peace" crooned in my ear: "Good intentions can be evil." Those we notice least, those who blend into the crowd, might one day stand beside us, might one day shake our hand—"Sometimes Satan comes as a man of peace. . . ."

And sometimes he comes as Hell's Angel.

PART
1

1

BORN THIS WAY

Outlaw is in my DNA.

—BIG PETE

My Outlaw training began with Risk: The Game of Global Domination, invented by French film director Albert Lamorisse and released as *La Conquête du Monde* ("The Conquest of the World").

We gathered nightly at the kitchen table beneath a bright suspended bulb—my mother, sister, brother, father—fiercely attentive, poised to attack. The strategy board game depicted a political map of the Earth, divided into forty-two territories, grouped into six continents. The goal was to occupy every space on the board, and necessarily, decimate the competition. Players controlled armies and used them to capture territories from other players, their fate determined by dice rolls.

"What do you want to be when you grow up?" My father grinned as I marched across his enemy lines.

"Boss."

I was only twelve.

I lived in a town of thirty-two thousand people on the outskirts of Wisconsin. My father probably thought I was just being cute. After all, most kids had delusions of grandeur. But I wasn't most kids. And I was hardly cute.

I was lucky my mom reminded me often. I got to keep my Christmas gifts every year.

The next night, my dad challenged me to a rematch, a game of chess. But in the quiet of our living room, amidst muffled farm sounds, I carefully used pawns to capture his knights and castles, and was dangerously close to snuffing out his king.

"Checkmate."

My father's face puffed red.

"How did you *do* that?"

And he and my mother fought . . . about chess moves. Glasses broke; pieces flew across the room, motionless pawns, like bleached plastic soldiers, scattered across the linoleum tiles.

"Peter, my Peter," my mom pleaded with me.

The fundamental flaw with chess was that a player had to sacrifice pieces (soldiers) to gain a tactical advantage.

I preferred the Chinese game Go; it involved takeover *without* sacrifice. Players took turns placing black and white stones in vacant spaces on a grid.

"And if a black piece lands horizontal to a white piece . . . ?" My father needed clarification.

"The opposite color takes away the other stone's liberty.

And when there are no liberties left, that stone can't stay on the board."

"So that's how you win?"

"Well . . . at the end of the game, there can be living *and* dead stones." I could see that I was losing him. "There are areas on the grid called forbidden points. . . ."

"How do you *win*?" He orbited around me.

"When both players *agree* the game's over, or when one player resigns."

"What?"

"Players can agree that stones that would have been inevitably captured are dead. And stones that cannot be captured are alive."

"Hey, punk, want to play a *real* game?" My uncle took me to the horse races.

He'd graduated third in his class from Marquette University, a private Catholic institution in Milwaukee, and became a CPA. But then he discovered the horses and his life "tumbled." When relatives spoke of Uncle Tony they lowered their voices, muttered phrases like "skid row" and "racetrack" and "broken promise." Then the aunts (mostly my mom) tried to "save him." They found him employment with Maidenform selling brassieres.

But when my uncle pulled up one morning in his marvelous Lincoln, I knew (even in the sixth grade) he no longer dabbled in ladies' underwear. He wore a long trench and expensive-looking shoes and his fingers sparkled with rings. He had made new "friends"—real gangsters who showed him how to make "real" money fixing horse races. My uncle showed me Chicago, a dazzling city that always smelled wet.

"Like money?" He took me to lunch at a fancy restaurant where the tables had stemmed glasses and cloth napkins, and the staff wore bow ties.

"There's a thirty-minute wait."

Uncle Tony slipped the host a few bills.

"Right this way."

"Watch and learn." My uncle motioned for me to follow.

I did. It didn't matter what he said. I saw what he did, and that mattered.

"Power plays happen at the subconscious level." He tore apart a bread roll. I sampled my unpronounceable dish and used all three forks. "When people feel powerful they stop trying to control themselves. You understand?"

Got it. No self-control.

We made many more trips to Chicago. And after a while the aunts stopped worrying he might be a "bad influence." My uncle plied them with carloads of beef, sweet peppers, and gravy. I watched. I learned. I wanted to be just like him.

"Play a real game with him," my mom pleaded with my uncle as she left for work one day.

"All my games are real." He winked at me, careful to pocket his dice and switch to Yahtzee when she returned.

At the horse races, I already knew from playing Monopoly and rolling dice that the odd number 7 was the most common roll and the color red the most landed-on property. I considered 7, Chance. If I rolled a 3, 7, or 9, I was most likely to land on a red property and avoid going to jail. So I bet on odds, put $300 on "Hurry Home Harry," a dark-horse contender, a real underdog, with a terrible chance at winning.

"Speed or skill has nothing to do with winning," my uncle mentored me. "A horse is judged by its comparison to the speed of *other* horses . . . and by its wins and losses."

We sat close enough to smell the dust from the track. Hooves thundered by, and my heart raced as I followed the progress of "Hurry Home Harry" on the backstretch. *Come on, come on, win!*

The bleachers rocked; spectators roared. My uncle waved his hands wildly in the air, never taking his eyes off his horse. The majestic beasts raced faster and faster, a blur of blinkers and shadow rolls. They resembled bandits racing from their locked gates—cloths across their noses blocked the track, prevented them from jumping shadows. They bolted sometimes two abreast, always in tight formation. Jockeys curled tight on their backs, whips in hand. Slashes of determination lined their faces.

"Hurry Home Harry," looking washed out, his mane sticky with sweat, galloped across the finish line.

"How'd you do, punk?"

"Great, really great. I made—"

My uncle put a finger to my lips. "A real man never talks about the money he's won or the women he's fucked."

Lesson learned. Nonetheless, I was so proud of my $3,000 winnings. Later, I learned my uncle had bet $44,000 on "Hurry Home Harry," a life's savings on a dark horse.

"Why . . . ?" I couldn't help myself.

"You need to keep your eyes open." My uncle tapped a finger to my forehead. "The skid row guys are there every day at that track, every day they're watching the horses race across that finish line. They know the score. They bet two dollars on 'Hurry Home Harry.'"

I still didn't get it.

"Because they have the most to lose, they're more likely to win."

Keep your eyes open. I did, but I wanted to do more than that: I wanted to see inside them, absorb their invisible intelligence.

I ran for student government . . . and lost.

"What happened?" my mom barked, hands on her hips. She looked disappointed.

"Nothing. I just wasn't good enough."

She marched over to me, cupped my chin in her hand, and uttered the words that would profoundly inform my life's path: "If you don't think you're number one, don't expect anyone else to think you're number one."

After that I left nothing to chance. I rigged every election—altar boy, student council, president of the Lettermen's Club. My uncle's words swirled in my head: "Perception is everything. It's what others see that matters."

I never did get to thank him. He "went away" suddenly—to a federal prison cell. It was somehow fitting. He had passed on his life's lessons. His utility had ended. People, after all, were just moveable game pieces. Some were destined to be pawns, a means to an end, while others would go on to be king.

I replaced Uncle Tony with the next best teacher, Mario Puzo's book *The Godfather*. Michael Corleone, the youngest son of the Mafia don, Vito Corleone, went to college. My uncle went to college. It was like a credential. I wanted that stamp of intelligence, not because I thought I would need it necessarily to become boss, but because I considered it a personal challenge and a social experiment with plenty of test subjects. (Never mind that I likely got into college because I played football.) I didn't realize I might actually have to study or that grades mattered to get a diploma. So when I was in danger of failing I came up with a plan. . . .

"List your major influences." The application for an internship with Wisconsin's speaker of the house had a host of ridiculous questions.

The Godfather was mandatory reading, like the Bible. I'd memorized key passages and phrases, having read the book seven times before the age of twenty. I graduated to Sun Tzu's *The Art of War,* Harry Truman's biography *Plain Speaking,* and finally to Robert Sabbag's *Snowblind,* which I credit to perfecting my considerable skills in the cocaine trade.

But somehow, I didn't think those references would impress. It was a big deal in my family that I attended (but found it unnecessary to graduate from) the University of Wisconsin—Whitewater with a bachelor's degree in political science.

"Why do you want this position?" The *real* answer? I needed the college credits to pull up my miserable GPA. But of course that's not what I wrote.

The job involved researching legislation to improve and

update small claims courts in Wisconsin. And the judge who led the charge happened to reside in Los Angeles. Judge Katsufracus (the original Judge Joseph Wapner) apparently informed the federal marshal who met me at the airport that "an important visiting dignitary from Wisconsin would be arriving."

"*You?*" The marshal lowered his sunglasses and arched a brow. "Somehow I thought you'd be a little older."

In his chambers, Judge Katsufracus squinted at me. His black robe spilled around him, making him look like a curtain with a head. "What do you want to do while you're here?"

"I like movies," I shrugged.

The judge smothered a smile. "I have a contact at Paramount."

In between working on legislation to improve the process of "burden of proof," I visited the set of *Moses* and watched the Red Sea part, I straddled the motorcycle "The Fonz" rode, and shook Wonder Woman's hand.

I pulled up my GPA and had enough credits to graduate.

"Now what?" I asked my father.

He didn't know. But one day he surprised me in our garage. I was in the middle of sawing a cue stick in half. He glanced behind me at the packed bag of clothing and asked,

"Are you on the run?"

"Not yet," I said. "But I'm moving to Dallas."

"Why?"

"It's closer to the Mexican border."

While the thought of making a go at drug trafficking,

even heading a cartel, sounded attractive, I wanted nothing to interfere with my plans to be the Boss of Chicago. So when the Feds paid me a visit in college and warned me about being an *un*charged coconspirator in a drug trafficking case, I didn't need further details.

Prison was not part of my grand plan. I didn't want to be a criminal by trade. "Outlaw" and "criminal" were not necessarily synonymous. Drug trafficking was a liability; I could never completely control the dealers or stop them from becoming users.

So I hid in a posh lake house I couldn't afford and each morning exchanged $20 bills for quarters, so I could access a pay phone on a moment's notice. I never called anyone from the same phone twice, nor more than once in the same day. This is how I avoided the Feds' suspicion and protected my drug dealers' identities.

Safety always; it was a mantra drilled into me from birth, when my mother pinned a blue bead to my pillow and insisted the "evil eye" would *protect me against bad spirits.* I'm pretty sure she didn't mean the Feds. Still, for years I carried a blue bead in my pocket . . . *just in case.* But the morning I accidentally broke a bathroom mirror, I considered other options (after all, I wasn't about to stop leading a dangerous life), even a blue eye tattoo on the back of my neck just below my hairline. But my mother's frantic voice replayed in my ear: "Peter, my Peter, please no ink."

I had often fantasized about my tombstone and the simple words I wanted carved below my name: *"Here Rests a Motherfucker."* But I respected my mom. No tattoos.

My future flashed before me one rainy midnight as two motorcyclists crested a hill, their bikes moving in unison like extensions of their bodies. Grace, power, and speed zigzagged through stalled cars and maneuvered potholes. Grinning skulls flapped on their back jackets.

But I wasn't finished running.

I disappeared for eight years, moving from city to city, sleeping in hotels, on park benches, homeless, honing my skills as a hustler. Until one day my mom called.

"Your cousin has a job for you." She sounded breathless, excited.

"I don't want a job."

"Please." She was near tears. "You can't live like this forever."

I hated that she worried. Truth be told, I didn't think I could ever get a job. I flunked a psych test once for a big corporate firm.

"We would never hire you," the recruiter said. "Your scores are off the charts."

"Too smart?" I hoped.

"Too scary."

"Scary good?"

"Is there such a thing?"

The problem, he elaborated, was that I could not be controlled. *I relented.* I accepted a position in a quality control lab in a chemical plant. The company made wax additives for the printing industry, for magazines like *Playboy* and *GQ,* so the ink wouldn't smear.

After several months working alongside chemists, I became the plant's manager and earned a decent salary. But I atrophied; I was not destined to be Ordinary.

"You don't fit in this place," a coworker remarked one morning.

"Sure I do."

He shook his head. "Nope. You're *resting*. I know people like you. You're waiting for the right time to escape."

He had a point.

I called a lawyer buddy of mine. "I need an adventure."

"Is that code for new motorcycle?" He laughed.

The Evolution engine had returned to the Harley-Davidson. No more "Shovelhead" trouble heads. I bought a new bike, and for the first time in years I exhaled.

Then fate intervened.

"You should come to the Moose Lodge," a friend suggested. *What the hell was that?*

"The Loyal Order of Moose; it's a fraternal service organization. They're having a dinner. . . ."

The Lodge, a palatial two-story building with a spacious dining area, kitchen, and bar on the first level and offices tucked upstairs, made a perfect clubhouse.

But first things first: I had to become a member of the Loyal Order of Moose—the LOM.

And so, after several more dinners at the lodge, I participated in a forty-five-minute initiation ritual for the Order.

I wore a loud Hawaiian shirt and boat shoes; the Moose wore matching yellow suits and ties and eyed me warily. The governor of the lodge asked the sergeant-at-arms to administer the Moose obligation.

"Do you believe in a Supreme Being?" he began.

Sure.

"Place your left hand over your heart and raise your right. Do you promise not to communicate or disclose or give any information—concerning anything—you may hereafter hear, see, or experience in this lodge or in any other lodge?"

Sure.

I was then directed to face Mooseheart (Illinois), bow my head, and mumble a silent prayer in what members called "the 9 O'Clock Ceremony."

"Suffer little children," I mindlessly repeated under my breath, "to come unto me and forbid them not, for such is the Kingdom of Heaven. God bless Mooseheart."

"The children of Mooseheart are supposed to kneel at their bedside in prayers as well," the lodge chaplain explained before he launched into the ten "thou shalts."

"Thou shalt believe in God and worship Him as thy conscience dictates," he ordered. "Thou shalt be tolerant to let others worship each in his own way." Other "thou shalts" pertained to patriotism, service to fellowmen, protection of the weak, avoidance of slander against a brother Moose, love of the LOM, faithfulness, and humility.

The governor grasped my hand while the members sang "Blest Be the Tie That Binds." Meanwhile, my thoughts spun into forming my *own* club, and how I could best gain control of the Loyal Order of Moose to accomplish this goal. The governor administered the second part of the obligation: "Do you promise to support Mooseheart, Moosehaven [a retirement community in Florida], help fellow Moose, settle disputes within the Order, and not join any unauthorized Moose organizations?" *Absolutely.* The prelate offered another prayer at the altar, and I joined in singing "Friendship We Now Extend."

Being a Moose was all well and good, but if I was to control the lodge and, more important, the treasury, I had to hold an officer's position. And that was only going to happen if I had sufficient votes. Typically only five members ever decided anything of importance (the same was true when I interned for the state legislature). The same five people showed up and formed "the Majority." I couldn't risk five people deciding *my* fate. So I recruited *thirty*-five of my loyal friends and indoctrinated them into the Loyal Order of Moose.

"How long do we have to do this?" one of them complained.

"Long enough to vote."

The governor was perplexed. It was "unheard of" to attract so many Moose in such a short period of time. The lodge had an incentives system: If a member recruited three prospects in a month he received a pin; five, a watch; *thirty-five,* a Palm Beach sports jacket. I quickly became a marvel in the Moose world—"exemplary Moose material."

Thirty-five votes later, I became the governor.

"I'm forming my own club," I announced one night at dinner.

"You mean a club within a club?"

"Yeah, something like that. I'm going to call it the Loyal Order, like the Loyal Order of Moose."

I had already designed the colors. The top rocker was going to be black and embroidered with "The Loyal Order," the bottom rocker silver with "Illinois" (because The Outlaws already claimed "Chicago" and would never approve), and on the centerpiece, a gold crest. I added intrigue with swords and skulls, a random #8, and a death card.

"Who're you going to recruit?"

"Moose."

"And Women of the Moose?" Debbie, my ol' lady, chimed in.

Well, it could never be 50/50. In any organization or partnership it could only ever be 49/51. In fact, Debbie would only ever make 49 percent of all significant decisions; 51 percent of the time the hard calls, the unpopular votes, the truly gut-wrenching judgments would be mine.

Equality didn't exist. It couldn't.

Women of the Moose received a special handbook with resources to help them become independent and productive. But broads didn't need a *handbook*. They, like everyone else, got what they *earned*.

2

LET THE GAMES BEGIN

A word of advice: We're in Chicago, just don't kill anyone.

—GREASED LIGHTNING

The Spanish word "adios" means "goodbye." In Outlaw-speak, it means "Angels Die in Outlaw States." The American Outlaws Association (AOA), established in 1965, has chapters worldwide and throughout the United States, with most grouped according to color-coded region: white for Illinois, gold for Wisconsin, orange for Florida, gray for Kentucky and Tennessee, silver for Georgia and Alabama, copper for the Carolinas, black for Ohio and Indiana, blue for Pennsylvania, red for New England and a few chapters in Philadelphia (because Philadelphia also has Angels, Pagans, and Warlocks). The *Chicago* Outlaws Motorcycle Club (aka OMG) is split into three parts: the South Side (the mother chapter), West Side, and North Side. "Patching in" to the

Outlaws involves sponsorship, months of probating (a fancy word for slavery), and mastering the club's playbook.

The goal of every game, after all, is winning. The rules are simple: Stop (insert: *kill*) any player (insert: *enemy*) whose mission interferes with complete domination. The roles: pawns (insert: *expendables*), soldiers (*well trained*), enforcers (insert: *loyal robots*), and kings (insert: *leaders;* insert: *Boss*). The Fight: turf. *Cripple or Kill. Cripple or Kill. Hells Angels.* Simple enough. The slogan encouraged a hunter/prey (human/animal) mentality. Outlaws viewed life through the sights of a rifle.

In fact, the escalating violence was reported as a series of "conflicts between Chicago-area Outlaws and Hells Angels motorcycle clubs. This growing feud [was] the result of a territorial conflict involving the conversion of Hell's Henchmen Motorcycle Club to Hells Angels. The Outlaws [were] vehemently opposed to the Hells Angels' establishing a Midwest chapter and [were] aggressively protecting their territory. To date, as a result of this feud, there have been three documented homicides and six bombings in a three-state area."[*]

By 1994, Taco Bowman, the Outlaws international president, led the charge when he ordered Outlaw Regional Boss Peter Rogers, aka Grease or Greased Lightning, to bomb the Hell's Henchmen, a Hells Angels–backed biker gang based

---

[*] Petersen, James R., *Playboy*, November 1, 2000, "The Biker Wars: Bar Fights, Car Bombings and Cold-Blooded Murder—It Was a Local but Brutal Conflict Between the Outlaws and the Hells Angels"

in Illinois. But when Grease hesitated, Taco moved to "Plan B" and commissioned other Outlaws to launch the assault "as soon as possible." He ordered more firebombings against Hells Angels clubhouses.

And for his small part in Taco's campaign of violence, Grease took a bullet in the leg and gut as he rode his Harley-Davidson on the Dan Ryan Expressway in Chicago. And though there were no suspects, word of the shooting spread throughout the Midwest, and the next day, the Outlaws targeted Rockford, Illinois, and a motorcycle shop owned by a Hell's Henchman. Kevin "Spike" O'Neill, the president of the Wisconsin/Stateline chapter of the Outlaws, gave the prospective assailant specific instructions to "do what you can," if "opportunity arose."

Spike's recruit, a wannabe Outlaw from the Insanity Motorcycle Club, understood completely. He entered the motorcycle shop, opened fire with his .45, then bludgeoned the victim with the butt of his gun. He then stabbed the victim again and again in the throat with a screwdriver and later reported to Spike that the "head gasket was blown . . . [and] leaking like a sieve." Spike rewarded him with membership and a belt buckle engraved with twin SS lightning bolts.

That kind of loyalty was rare, found only in fraternal groups, among like-minded brothers who pledged allegiance to one another to honor, respect, and *kill* if necessary for the privilege of wearing the patch. It was an honor among thieves.

An honor I understood and aspired to achieve. But first,

I needed a way in. As president of the Loyal Order, I had instant legitimacy in the OMG world. The fact that I also had an intimate knowledge of the drug trade was a bonus. But being a member of my own club was not going to land me the position of Boss of Chicago. For that title, I had to control the club that controlled the city. I needed to fortify my position, align with the Outlaws, occupy territories, eliminate opponents, and befriend the leader.

I paced Grease's dirty, gray hospital room. Recessed lights flickered on the ceiling. Blood spotted his sheets. Part of his guts seeped out of his stomach. Feeding tubes snaked through his nose.

"We're going to get the motherfuckers who did this to you," his guards promised him.

I offered to drive. It may not have been the most glamorous entry into the Outlaws' "inner sanctum," but the position kept me close to Grease.

"I *could* use your help," Grease said once he'd recovered, though *plumbing* was not exactly the job I'd envisioned.

We drove into Chinatown past rows of dried fish heads and blue live crabs. Red paper lanterns spun in the wind. We pulled up to a framed bamboo restaurant with a red dragon fountain. The owner waved us in. "Water everywhere," he said in broken English.

"Get the router." Grease headed to the basement. The ceiling buckled.

The doors to the van swung wide over a deep puddle. My boots filled with debris. I retrieved the equipment and joined Grease inside. Smells of raw sewage and food waste made my eyes tear. Grease drained the pipes and twenty minutes later announced, "I fix it."

He ordered a plate of chicken dumplings and a side of white rice. The owner slapped cash into Grease's hand and I returned to the van with the router, wading back through the puddles, my socks sucking like sponges inside my boots.

Grease hobbled into the passenger's seat, his legs skimming the floor, and I clicked on the engine. "Get my lunch."

The owner looked agitated "You no fix."

"Grease?"

He winked at me. "I fix."

"I pay you but you no fix."

I shut off the engine; Grease struggled out of the van. "Get the router," he said. "Watch and learn," and disappeared inside. Again, I waded through mud puddles and retrieved the equipment, then brought it inside and watched as Grease injected special drain-cleaning enzymes into the clogged pipes.

"*Now* it's fixed." He demanded payment.

"I already pay you." The owner shook his head.

"Take care of this, will you?" Grease grabbed his bag of steamed dumplings and white rice and headed back to the van.

"That was for the first job." I figured this was my learning curve.

The owner opened his mouth to protest, but I shut him up. "Look, if you don't pay, I'll beat your fucking brains in and then I'll just take your money anyway."

Chinaman blanched. Suddenly he understood perfect

English. He reached into his pocket for another wad of cash. I didn't need to count the money—every bill weighed a gram.

Grease popped a dumpling into his mouth, chewed slowly, noted the "slippery texture," and snatched the cash from my hand. No "Thank you." No percentage for my help. He ate his dinner in silence, counting the dumplings, alternating them between bites of rice. And when he finished, he carefully folded the empty bag and tucked it into the crack in his seat next to several other folded paper bags.

"You should come to dinner next week." He licked his fingers, and I knew that was the closest he would ever come to gratitude.

We met in Chinatown, 6:30 sharp. Serious gangsters dined at the Ling Ling restaurant—Outfit, Outlaws . . . even, on occasion, cops. We occupied the upstairs. We were an unusually large crowd, ten couples squeezed into a corner room draped with red velvet curtains. As the only non-Outlaw at the table, I felt privileged and honored to be included among Grease's elite.

But this wasn't just "dinner" for me—it was opportunity. I needed to know just how much control over Grease I really had. Phrases from *The Godfather* rolled like credits in my head, including something about "Control the man at the top and you become the man at the top." As my first test, I suggested Grease change the channel on the television to the Stanley Cup Finals. Sports provided a natural bridge, a universal code among men, with an immediately applicable vocabulary: "teams," "rivals," "rules," "goals," "turf," "weapons." In ice hockey, as in the Outlaws, as in life, each player had a specific position and job. The job of offense, for instance, was to score goals. The defense was there to protect the goal. I hadn't yet decided my role.

Grease snapped his fingers at the waiter, whom he called "Tom" despite his name tag. The same principle applied: "defenseman," "right wing," "left wing," "center"—didn't matter. It was "Tom's" job to switch the channel. "Score."

The couples ordered a feast: twelve entrees, including crabs, shrimp, and lobster tails dribbled with plum sauce. Tom repeated the orders back, asking at least twice about white rice. He jotted nothing down. His large glasses slipped to the edge of his nose. Grease handed him the menus.

"Your buddy's back in town." Dominic played with his chopsticks. His beard skimmed his plate. A scar on his right cheek puckered like a butthole. He wore a smashed bullet on a chain around his neck.

Backlash, Grease's enforcer, studied Dominic as if he were a fly he wanted to pop.

"I'm just the messenger." Dominic put up his hands. And I learned quickly that in his world "messenger" meant target practice.

Backlash zoomed from zero to fifty in seconds. "Want to deliver one from me?"

Click.

Fear skittered across Debbie's face. I felt a little guilty. Chinatown was about making connections, face time over dinner with important Outlaw chapter officers and high-ranking soldiers.

"You mean the one who looks like a Keebler Elf?" Debbie remarked once about Grease.

"Yes. That one."

Click. Click. Click. A chorus of revolvers resounded underneath the table. Adrenaline shot through me. My first Chinatown dinner over in seconds, like some weird sequel to Chicago's "Bloody Valentine Massacre."

"Knock it off." Grease tapped his fork against his porcelain teacup. He seemed strangely unfazed by the violent outburst—odd, considering he was still recovering from bullet wounds.

Dominic threw down his napkin, stood, his gun cocked in one hand. He tapped his date with the barrel. "Let's go."

Backlash shot to his feet. "We're leaving too."

The last couple scraped back their chairs, folded their napkins, and promptly left. Grease seemed unconcerned by the sudden departures. Debbie squirmed a little, sipped her warm water, and nibbled on the lemon rind. "Tom" filled the awkward silence, balancing several trays of food on his arms and placing the silver-covered dishes on the table. Grease lifted each lid, billowy steam enveloping him as he sampled them, seemingly oblivious that Debbie and I remained.

"There's too much food." Grease ordered "Tom" to pack up the leftovers in "takey homey" boxes.

"I insist you have some." He handed me several containers.

"Grease never shares," I confided later to Debbie. "This is
huge." It was a major breakthrough. Grease trusted me,
considered me a friend.

She unpacked the boxes on the counter. "What do you
want me to do with these?"

"Is anything salvageable?"

She peered inside the cartons, stiffened, and said with
her back to me, "We might have a problem."

"What's wrong?"

"He gave us ten boxes of white rice."

*This was bad. This was really bad. My path into the
Outlaws hinged on this.* If Grease thought for one minute
we had taken his rice . . .

"Don't say a fucking word," I cautioned Debbie as we headed
to Chinatown the next Friday.

"You think he's even going to ask?"

"He's going to ask."

"Why would he care?"

"Trust me, he's going to care."

We sat down at 6:30 sharp again. The guests at the
table had thinned, mostly Outfit guys with their ol' ladies.
Grease insisted "Tom" switch the channel on the television
to the game. He caught the waiter by his elbow and said,
"You makey mistakey."

The waiter frowned. He was not the same "Tom" from

the week before. Debbie met my gaze across the table. There was a slight tick in her jaw. My thoughts raced—*Don't you say a fucking word.* This was self-preservation.

"Tom" took the fall. Tension cut across the table. Grease stared icily at the waiter.

The waiter giggled nervously. He had a slight tremor in his hand.

"You forgot my rice." Grease's tone sent a chill down my spine. He flapped open his cloth napkin, tucked an end into the neck of his T-shirt, and placed his gun on the table.

"You want more?"

"Last week." Grease tapped a finger on the gun butt and repeated the words slowly, as if he were communicating in code. "Rice. Forgot?"

"OK, I bring now."

That night I drove Grease home, helped him with the "takey homey" boxes. Heavy curtains draped his front windows. Madame Cherie, his ol' lady, buzzed the garage open; a narrow path tunneled through stacks of canned goods, bike parts, discarded and broken appliances, and bags and bags of garbage.

3

MY PLAYBOOK

Wounded people are dangerous—they know they can survive.

—BIG PETE

College football (which I once played) was a game of inches. Sometimes that's all that was needed, a couple of inches to execute a well-calculated goal. No more rice mix-ups. No more volatility involving tempers and potential bullet spray, reminiscent of the Ling Ling dining experience.

It was my move. I wanted (notice I did not say "need") the Outlaws' trust and respect. Name recognition was critical to my overall success. "Outlaw" opened doors. I planned a large party. My wedding to Debbie (aka "Bun"), held in the Grand Ballroom of the Willowbrook Holiday Inn, was an Event.

Guests included Moose members, country line-dancers, the Loyal Order, and various motorcycle clubs, including the Chicago Outlaws. I spent days devising elaborate seating charts so rivals did not share tables, feuding Bosses kept a healthy distance, and club politics did not erupt into dangerous debate.

"This is like seating for the UN," I told Debbie.

Debbie's wedding

"And you haven't even addressed our parents and relatives." *True. Hers were cultured figurines, mine . . . very loud.*

Guests arrived from the service at the Greek Orthodox church in individual limousines and gathered in the atrium of the hotel until the ballroom opened. Debbie's mom clutched her purse tightly to her chest, looking wan, trying to fade into the walls. Madame Cherie, Grease's old lady (an ex-stripper once married to a cop), stood next to her, reeking of weed and gardenias, barely contained in her rose bustier, probably secretly hoping this wasn't going to be another biker wedding, with paper plates and plastic forks.

I had ordered a live band from Nashville and a local disc jockey to play Marshall Tucker and other personal favorites. But when I showed him my playlist, he balked, pissing me off.

As I stormed out of the ballroom into the atrium, the doors smacked Backlash in the face. Once convicted of manslaughter for murdering two Latin Kings over donuts, he was a member of the Joliet chapter of the Outlaws Motorcycle Club and the Chicago Boss's enforcer. Backlash appeared at my wedding clean-shaven, hair clipped, "so [he could] walk amongst the squares." He took the cue and headed into the ballroom to have a chat with the DJ.

"Look at me." Backlash snapped his fingers at him; the DJ's hands trembled. "Play anything Peter doesn't like and I'll slit your fucking throat."

The DJ's voice cracked as he announced the bridal party, and Debbie and I waded through billowing smoke from a machine to the "Peter Gunn Theme." And when the band finally arrived, the DJ disappeared, leaving behind his equipment.

Later his supervisor called me. "You're not going to . . . *harm* him, are you?" Don't get me wrong: I would have, and I would have enjoyed it, but it was enough that Backlash had threatened him with bodily harm. To have someone of Backlash's caliber step in as enforcer on my behalf was huge. We weren't even in the same club, but he already viewed me as a Boss.

Amidst plumes of weed and table dancing, waiters served filet mignon on plates with delicate gold piping. Backlash danced with my mom while the rest of my family bickered loudly over the guests' fashion choices and the number of shots they could swallow. Meanwhile, Debbie's parents sat quietly at a corner table, looking wan and pale, pretty cloth napkins spread across their laps.

Cops swarmed the hotel near midnight and politely suggested we "wrap things up." But when Backlash demanded another Crown Royal after the open bar closed, I slipped the bartender a $100 bill for the whole bottle and warned him, "It might be best to just keep Backlash happy."

"Grease needs you at the docks to help with his boat," Backlash called to tell me a few days later. "Help" was code for "work." And "boat" was a stretch. I actually doubted the fucking thing floated. Hardly seaworthy, the craft fit on the back of a trailer. Grease liked to drift in the lagoons.

"It's where he thinks," Backlash said. "Or, just smokes weed."

The sky was gray and overcast; whitecaps split the water. A line was formed on the dock. Seagulls glided overhead, diving into the choppy cold for fish. Backlash waved me over.

Grease paced the wooden jetty, hands shoved into the pockets of his bib overalls. The Chicago skyline jutted in the distance. Clouds circled above large metallic and stone columns. We shivered, blew into our cupped hands, waited for the line to move. The first drops of rain plopped on Grease's boat. Then, the man behind us cut in front. Just like that, his fate was sealed.

Backlash sprung to action—a bowie knife flashed in one hand, his other squeezed the man's throat. The line behind me suddenly thinned; people scattered, yelps and gasps punctuating the gloom. One family dropped their picnic basket and littered the deck with ham-and-cheese sandwiches; gulls swooped down and picked apart the insides.

"I'll cut your fucking throat." The man's eyes bulged as Backlash skimmed the blade across his flesh and drew blood. *Jesus, he was really going to kill him.*

Grease screamed, "Stop!"

Then, as if snapped out of a trance, Backlash released his grip. The man dropped to the dock, sputtering, coughing, barely able to stand. Backlash's thumb had left an imprint on the man's throat. We bolted just as sirens screeched the air.

"Peter," Backlash called me later, his voice sounding thin. "They're coming for me."

He was in full-blown panic.

"I have to go out," I said to Debbie; she knew better than to ask for details. By the time I arrived at Backlash's place, he had spread his arsenal of weapons over the bedroom floor: grenades, Molotov cocktails, chains, brass knuckles, and assorted pistols. He paced, twirling a Glock around his middle finger.

"They're coming." He watched the empty street. *He was really freaking me out.* He lived alone but had multiple offspring . . . somewhere. His breathing was labored. I thought he might pass out, or worse—shoot something. I didn't know what to do really, so I invited him to dinner.

"Bun will make your favorite."

He relaxed a bit, his strange, flat eyes crinkling at the edges.

"I like you, Peter." *Score.*

Wind blew through the streets, sliced through the empty buildings. I mounted my bike, inhaled the darkness. I liked him too. He represented all I ever wanted to be: a rebel, a nonconformist, a detached and potentially limitless destructive force hovering on the fringes of society, completely and utterly free. My dark mirror.

One play deserved another, and that weekend Backlash invited me to an "Outlaw National," held in Joliet at the Chicagoland Speedway, "in honor of West Side Tommy, murdered" just a few days before. We parked our bikes next to flatbed trailers, SUVs, RVs, and campers along Gecko Ridge, so close to the track we could smell the burning rubber. At dusk, as barbecues fired up and Outlaws settled in with cold beers, Backlash paced, his boots crunching in the gravel.

"I need something," he said. "Peter . . ."

I knew he meant blow. But this was Joliet, unfamiliar territory. My contacts lived in Chicago. This was a test.

"I'm sure you can work something out," Backlash said as he leaned against his car, anxious and sweaty, looking like he had been up all night.

Loud music blared over the speakers.

I made a phone call. My connection referred me to *his* sources.

"You've met him?" I asked.

"Yeah, sure."

"You'll let him know I'm coming?" *Click.*

I headed out to Bolingbrook, a ghetto similar to Englewood in Chicago. The dealer lived in a run-down olive green two-story with a broken tricycle on the front lawn. I arrived alone; it was the only way I could be sure to avoid witnesses.

I knocked, and chipped paint flecked off a rotting panel. Several slides and clicks later, the front door cracked open. The place smelled like a dentist's office.

"I don't know you." The dealer motioned for me to sit in his kitchen. Shirtless and sweaty, he opened the pantry, flashing shelves of assault rifles balanced above bags of flour.

"Jose sent me." My mouth was dry, the tips of my fingers numb.

"How do *I* know Jose sent you? How do I know you know Jose?" His voice sounded scratchy and his nose kept running. Small pipes fashioned out of soda cans lined the sink. I had a bad feeling about this.

"Look." I pushed back from the table. "Jose said you could hook me up. If that's not true, I'm out of here." The dealer whipped out his Glock and waved it at me. "You'll leave when I tell you to leave."

I stared at his shaking hands. The room suddenly shrunk. "What are you going to do?" *In retrospect, that probably wasn't my best line. Never bait a dealer who's been awake for days.*

"Why so rushed?" The dealer flirted with the trigger. He peered into the street. "You bring the Feds? Are you a Fed?" He pressed the Glock to my temple. "Give me one reason why I shouldn't blow your fucking brains out."

"Call Jose." I swallowed. "See if I check out."

"Fuck you!" he yelled in my ear. "You don't give me orders."

I inhaled slowly. *I didn't have time for this shit. By now Backlash had probably imploded. I was there to buy an* *ounce of coke, worth at most $1,000.* I had orchestrated hundreds of deals before, without incident. But this dealer had violated the rules of play—he *used*. This made him paranoid and sloppy.

I knew how to cut coke, add weight without adding mass. It was the difference between a pound of lead and a pound of feathers. In the end, both equaled a pound, but a pound of lead was the size of a fist and feathers could fill a gunnysack. It was easy to add grams of coke to feathers. No one dealt pure cocaine unless he was El Chapo. I knew how to break down coke, add to it, and re-rock the drug for a bargain.

The dealer flipped open his burner phone and dialed Jose. Tomato sauce congealed on two plates in the sink. A fly buzzed in the faucet. *There was no way I was going to fucking die here with my brains splattered on these checkered tiles miles from Chicago.* My heart raced. After a few more minutes of silence, the dealer pocketed his Glock and tossed me a baggie of coke.

"What took you so long?" Backlash trotted off behind a trailer to make his own sale. He returned minutes later and slapped a few bills in my hand.

Cheers erupted from the speedway. Backlash popped a can of beer, chatted with me about his son, whom he affectionately called "The Professor."

"He's so smart." Backlash pressed the cold can to his forehead and laughed. "He'll probably become a cop."

"Hey." Footsteps crunched behind us.

"What do you want?" Backlash gulped the last of his beer and crushed the can with his head.

The buyer waved the baggie of coke at Backlash. "You're short."

"Short?"

"Yeah, you shorted me."

"Peter." Backlash waved me over, rolled his eyes. "He wants his fifty bucks back."

"I didn't short him." I shoved a hand in my pocket to retrieve the cash and heard the sound of ribs crack. Backlash had punched the buyer, knocking him to the ground, and now he was slamming his skull into the dirt. The buyer yanked a clump of Backlash's hair and pulled him down. A crowd circled the sweaty mass. No one intervened. Finally, an Outlaw regional enforcer stepped in, but before he could pry the two apart, Backlash had reached for his serrated bowie knife and stabbed the enforcer with the precision and speed of an assassin.

"The fucker tried to kill me." Backlash looked a little dazed as Outlaws swarmed him and dragged him inside a trailer. One wiped the blood from his blade with a rag. Another helped the enforcer to the curb and waited with him until the ambulance arrived.

All this over $50?

"Want a cookie?" An Outlaw named Truck stoked hot coals near the trailer.

"What?"

He shook a plate at me. "These are magic cookies. They'll take the edge off."

I popped one in my mouth. And soon the night sky filled with tiny fireflies. The dark puddles of blood became hard stones. A strange calm filled me.

Truck's laugh echoed. "It's all good, right?"

Suddenly I was on my bike, blowing down dark streets, his whisper in my head: *It's all good—right*. . . .

The next day Backlash came to dinner. Debbie and I tried not to stare as he sliced up his plate of dolmades.* He was on the phone, cradling it between his ear and shoulder as he slowly chewed. After several minutes he handed me the receiver, wiped the oil from his hands with a napkin, and pushed back from the table.

"Peter, I have to go."

"What's happening?"

"Fuckers at the South Side are trying to oust Grease."

I didn't know exactly what that involved, but it sounded like mutiny. I was on my feet. "I'll go with you."

Backlash paced. "What do you have here?"

I retrieved a .40-caliber Glock from a shelf in the pantry and tucked a .38 snub nose into my waistband.

Debbie knew better than to say a word, but I knew she was worried. *Hell, I was worried.*

When we arrived at the South Side clubhouse, Backlash rang the bell. It sounded like a gong. It didn't matter that I was with the Loyal Order—Backlash and Grease were my friends. I was prepared to do anything necessary to protect them—even take a bullet. "Good," a brother said to me once we were inside and I'd slid onto a bar stool next to him

---

* Stuffed grape leaves

and told him as much. "That way when the shooting starts slugs will pass through you first before they ever strike me."

Once they were opened for us, Backlash pushed through the large swinging doors of the clubhouse toward the sound of yelling, furniture scraping against wood, glass shattering, and baseball bats being thwacked.

"What's going on in there?" I asked.

"They're discussing things."

My whole body tensed; I rested my finger on the trigger of my gun. No one spoke. Sounds muffled. The room filled with members; some played pool, their bodies framed in puffs of chalk, balls clacking against balls like gunshots. The scene was suspended animation, the lull before explosion.

Shot glasses shook. Broads huddled in a corner, one sucking the beads of her large plastic necklace. Another fiddled with her clumpy hair. They reminded me of dolls left out from vigorous play.

The back room was suddenly eerily quiet. I shifted on the stool, my right leg almost numb from the static. The gun warmed in my hand. I had never shot anyone, never killed anyone. The closest I had ever come to witnessing a murder was the man on the dock with Backlash's knife pressed against his throat.

Still, I'd never felt so alive. And whether it was the idea of dying or the thought of never having *really* lived before that terrified me more, I wasn't sure. But I had such clarity— the room, the lights, the bar flickered like the past fading in and out of focus. A fly buzzing on a shot glass sounded like a jet. My boots blended into the black floor. The jukebox played "Welcome to the Jungle," and Axl Rose's voice boomed to the ceiling, then whizzed from wall to wall. His was the sound of Power.

The back door swung open, and out walked two Outlaw brothers with Grease and Backlash in tow.

"Non-Outlaws need to leave." The Boss snapped his fingers at me. "We're about to start Church."

That's what they called their business meetings, reserved for full-patched members. I was reminded again that no matter what, no matter how close I became with the Outlaws, I was still an Outsider. *Still,* Bosses noticed me. And they noticed I'd come with Backlash.

Backlash came over the next day. "How about you and I take a ride?"

We sped down alleys and deserted streets. Thunder rumbled in the distance. A few slashes of lightning lit up the afternoon sky. Wind bit into my face. Backlash didn't speak. He didn't have to; we fell into a road rhythm, noting subtle changes in each other's throttle that signaled turning, slowing down, speeding up. He zigzagged between semis, and nearly clipped parked cars. I absorbed noise and smells through my skin, becoming part of the road.

By the time Backlash stopped, I was exhausted, having already had whole conversations with him in my head.

"They're not too happy with me." We were stopped on a ramp on the expressway, target practice for Hells Angels. He'd run out of gas. But I always traveled with an extra tank.

As Backlash filled up, he said, "At least Grease can stay

on medical. They're not going to make him retire." He opened the gym bag he always carried with him; it was filled with exotic sex toys, and for a minute I thought he might give me a token of his appreciation, but instead he pulled out a bungee cord, then secured the bag tighter.

"I did something," he said. "It was pretty fucking stupid." He never elaborated, and I'd learned not to ask for details. But I knew from biker-speak, and had heard enough through the grapevine, that he'd made a threat to two Regional Bosses. They had a reputation for ruthlessness and would never have been intimidated by Backlash (an enforcer from the Joliet chapter) unless . . . he had flashed a gun.

"At least you can brag that you were the last to ride with Backlash. If you want to be a *real* Outlaw, Peter, you have to keep the brothers safe. Not that I'm saying you should *kill* anyone." He chuckled. "Unless, of course, it's on purpose and you need to make a point. But do just enough to remind them that you're willing. And if it looks like you're going to go to prison, run."

Note taken. I had some rules of my own, specifically how *not* to get killed.

Pete's Rule #1: Study fingers. If a guy wears four rings more than likely he is unarmed—he won't be able to squeeze his finger through the pistol guard.

Pete's Rule #2: If a van has no lock on the outside, chances are good there are men positioned with Uzis on the inside, just waiting to fling open the door and fire.

Pete's Rule #3: Always hug the fast lane against the wall; if you ride in the middle, someone can pull up on either lane and gun you down.

Pete's Rule #4: Study the club you *want* to be most like and apply what you learn.

I studied the Hells Angels.

After all, the best defense is a good offense. The Hells Angels had only a nominal presence in Chicago, thanks to the Outlaws' "hush hush" elimination campaign. If given the opportunity, as one Outlaw unabashedly reported to the press, Outlaws were "to take a shot . . . try to kill [the Hells Angel] . . . go to other clubhouses [and plot ways] to burn 'em up, blow 'em up, shoot 'em up. That's just what hunters *do*."

The Hells Angels had no official clubhouses, only sporadic gatherings in local bars and restaurants downtown.

"There've been sightings" of Hells Angels, the Outlaws told me one day, adding that I should "collect intel, conduct reconnaissance, count heads, check rockers, report new, emerging support clubs." All with the underlying message: *Kill, kill, kill.*

A recent federal raid that had resulted in eleven Outlaw arrests and ninety-nine prosecutions for crimes (twelve of them cold-blooded murders) served as a sobering reminder of the brutality the Outlaws could inflict on the Hells Angels.

Three executions in particular, of Hells Angels roped to

cinder blocks and thrown into a rock pit, lingered in my mind. As did the brutalization of two of their ol' ladies, one shot in the head with a speargun, the other disemboweled, her body dragged from the back of a boat until it broke apart.

Little Tony held a gathering at the Paradise Inn. "Want to go to a party?" I asked Debbie. "We'll blend in better as a couple."

We dressed the part in silence. Meeting Little Tony required a certain panache: a plain black Harley T-shirt, no indicia of the Loyal Order. I needed to be ordinary, someone Little Tony believed he could intimidate. We climbed onto our bikes. Debbie fixed her bandanna, nodded. *Ready.* We communicated almost telepathically. And corny as it sounds, I cherished those ordinary fleeting moments when the masks slipped off, when we felt safe even as a bomb ticked softly under our skin. We shot off like two anxious teens on prom night.

We missed our turn, zoomed passed the Inn, drifted into the gore, and made a U-turn at a busy intersection. We crossed over four lanes of traffic. Horns honked. A few drivers flipped us off. When we finally arrived at the upscale sports bar, Little Tony greeted us warmly, slapped a beer in my hand, and introduced me to the handful of brothers. I nursed the beer, taking inventory, picking up details I could use: Tony had a sweaty grip, small scuff marks on his boots, a scratchy voice. He cleared his throat before he spoke. The television blared above him, flashing snippets of news clips:

random shootings, bar brawls, a headshot of a heavily tattooed convict sentenced to life in prison, reports of a gang "at large" responsible for "wildings," like life imitating art.

Several Invaders swiveled behind Little Tony on stools. They stared at Debbie, cannibalized her body, her beautiful, pale face. She studied stuck coins in the floor, careful to avoid eye contact. She played a part: an ornamental decoy. I resisted the urge to smash their heads into the counter. *Focus, focus, focus.*

Life was a series of chess moves; Little Tony and his supporters were mere pawns, and Debbie, my queen. Queens could be sacrificed if it meant the king's next move was checkmate. The more I sipped, the more Tony ordered shots, and it dawned on me: This meet and greet was not *my* audition, it was *his*. This was *his* show-and-tell. *I* made *him* look good.

"We could use a guy like you." Little Tony ordered another beer.

And *I* could use a guy like *him*.

4

THE LOYAL ORDER

I was a mythological figure.

—BIG PETE

The National Coalition of Motorcyclists (NCOM), founded in 1986, formed as a nationwide umbrella organization designed to join motorcycle groups, clubs, and associations for the purpose of mutual exchange of information, legislative strategy, and solidarity. With over two thousand members, the organization served as a united group run by bikers *for* bikers, with an eighteen-member board of directors representing nine geographic regions across the United States.

At NCOM conventions, patch-holder meetings opened with prayer and the Pledge of Allegiance (my hypocrisy only went so far). Awards presentations followed: trophies given for "oldest bike," "fastest bike," "best bike," and even "world's fastest probate*."

---

* A probationary member vying for full-patch status in the club.

Attorneys and lobbyists spoke and reviewed bikers' rights and explained relevant parts of the constitution. The goal of NCOM was to fight against biker discrimination through awareness and education. And those in attendance represented a strange amalgamation of one-percenter* and square; Outlaws, Bandidos, and Sons of Silence shared space with Free Masons, Leathernecks, Christian Unity Bikers, Bikers for Christ, and Soldiers for Jesus. Amidst raucous applause, we received "police harassment cards" to help us document patterns of abuse (*P.S.: These never worked*).

"If you get arrested," an attorney took the podium, "you'll want to give the department this." He flashed another card and read: "I [insert name] give [insert name] power of attorney to collect my shit and take possession of my bike, which is being held at [insert location]." (*P.S.: total bullshit*).

We learned about the First Amendment, freedom of speech and assembly.

"When you fly your patch, that is a form of speech," the lawyer continued. "When you get together at a meeting like this you are exercising your right to assemble." A few people clapped.

"You are also exercising that right when you go to a poker run or a rally or a fairground." More applause.

"We have done nothing wrong," a patched member said

---

* Outlaw motorcycle clubs are distinguished by a "1%er" diamond patch worn on the colors signifying the one percent of motorcyclists who disobey 99% of the laws.

as he pounded his fist on the podium. "But everywhere we go, we are persecuted. People are afraid of us. They say we carry weapons. How many of you are packing today?"

He raised his hand. No one in the audience joined in.

"I am," he shouted, and raised a copy of the Bible high over his head.

The crowd was on its feet, whooping, clapping. Some hollered "Amen," and another added, "We are armed with the constitution."

That night, I replayed footage from my favorite televangelist, Jim Bakker. I studied his perpetually sweaty face and marveled at his tearful delivery at the podium, the amazing passion in his voice as he rallied an audience of thousands. He used no notes, no prompter, and took no breaks. He cast a spell. I practiced dramatic pauses in the dark of my bedroom as parts of his famous speeches raced through my head.

And so when an Outlaw, Rider, approached me about a "little problem" he needed "handled," I was more than willing to oblige.

"It involves the Rebel Knights." The club's members were mostly cops. Rider and I met in a local bar, grabbed a cramped booth in the back, and ordered drinks. "The fuckers are trying to form a confederation of clubs, a small army of allies. If they succeed they will control all of Chicago." He swallowed his beer and said, "We have to do it first."

My body tingled at the very prospect of power and control. I appreciated how he included me in his "we."

"The *problem*"—Rider wiped the back of his mouth with his hand—"is that we have to be discreet, stealthlike—we can't make it *look* like the Outlaws are in charge. I mean we're not fucking bullies, right?" He let out a belly laugh. Sweat slid down the side of his cheek. *Hell no.* He leaned in close, narrowed his gaze, I could tell he was going to ask me something important.

"The Outlaws need a chairman—*you.*" He pointed his finger at my chest and ordered another beer. He could barely sit still. "We need you to appear neutral. You're a Loyal Order. If you're in charge, you can convey the message to the other clubs that they are either going to support the Outlaws or they're not going to exist."

That sounded reasonable enough.

Rider's plan was brilliant—not the Outlaw part, but the me-as-chairman part. As the designated leader of the confederation of clubs, I would gain instant credibility with the Outlaws while also converting and recruiting a city of loyal supporters who would ultimately pledge their allegiance to *me.*

It was my way in.

"We would be in charge, only *not* in charge because *you* would be in charge," Rider repeated.

I would be in charge, all right . . . of the whole fucking city.

My COC—Confederation of Clubs—would be like a mini United States, an extension of NCOM.

I orchestrated the first meeting at the Moose Lodge and, in the spirit of NCOM, invited a virtual "Who's Who" of motorcycle clubs in the Chicagoland area, including the DC Eagles, Fugarwe Tribe, Brothers Rising, Rebel Knights, the Outlaws, the Hells Angels, and Mextecas, even black and Polish clubs like the Hell's Lovers, Sokol Riders, and Legacy made the list. The rules (which I wrote) permitted each club to send its Boss and two patched members to the meeting. The goal: unification. The clubs were meant to meet once a month to fight discrimination against patch-holders.

"They're arriving." The Outlaw named Jaws peered into the street, the parking lot already overrun with Outlaws. By this time the club had left NCOM (citing "security concerns").

"No one gets frisked," I reminded him.

"What if they're packing?"

"No one gets frisked." I hoped to convey an atmosphere of mutual trust.

But within minutes of the respective Bosses convening in the Moose Lodge, conflict erupted.

"Rebel Knights have cops in their club," a DC Eagle said, looking like a racehorse ready to charge the starting gate. He refused to sit at a table with the Rebel Knights' Boss—a sergeant who headed the organized crime unit of the Chicago Police Department. The DC Eagle paced, snorted, looked like he was ready to bolt.

Little Tony arrived with an entourage of two; his eyes bugged when he saw me dressed as a Loyal Order with an Outlaw support patch. He hesitated in front of me, shook his head. No one mingled. No one veered far from his own club. Everyone stood ready to put a bullet in his rival.

"This is going well," Jaws said under his breath. After a few more minutes of tense silence, the National Boss of the DC Eagles stepped forward to lead the meeting.

"Get the fuck back," the Outlaw Poison said, and slammed the Eagle's head into a glass sliding door; a loud crack resounded. And the scene unfolded like a movie montage of my own re-creation: rival biker gangs squaring off, neck veins bulging, eyes popping with rage. I envisioned the cameras slowly circling the room, zooming in on everyone's face, everyone's back.

Then Cal, the director (some neutral peacemaker) yelled, "Cut!" No one moved. Most clubs subscribed to an "all on one" philosophy; fight rules were memorialized in club charters, penned as bylaws: "When one fights, we all fight." Fists flew reflexively. Assault "victims" didn't exist; offenders (all of us gangsters) expected to fight. In fact, under my direction the scene would have gone something like this: thrashing bodies, fists and boots to skulls, and, in the end, a Buck knife jammed into the losing offender's throat.

Blood sprayed across the tiles. A speck stained the shirt of Vito, an old gangster who worked as a spy for the Creative Underground. The DC Eagles' Boss, doubled over, moaned, held his nose; it began to swell and bruise.

Calmly, Vito walked behind the bar, wet a towel, and dabbed at the spatter on his shirt.

Sirens ripped into the night. *Shit, my first meeting and we were all going to jail.*

"Better mop that up." Vito tossed the towel to the DC Eagle.

"Got a place to hide?" I asked. Jaws ushered me toward the back of the room.

Minutes later, all of us had squeezed into a tiny crawl space behind the stage on the second floor, united briefly against a common enemy: the cops. Hells Angels mashed against Outlaws; Rebel Knights pressed shoulder to shoulder with Hells Angels. DC Eagles shared space with Shines. Guns and knives cut into our waistbands. I gulped dry air like a guppy in a shallow fish tank. Bodies were too close. *This wasn't at all how I envisioned my COC.* The DC Eagle with the cracked nose turned a slight shade of purple, and my thoughts became consumed with the blood on the floor.

Little Tony's face pressed so close to mine we both narrowed our gaze to a bug wedged into the grout as we listened to footsteps below us, chairs scraping, sirens, and loud commands.

"We should do this again soon," Jaws said.

I planned on it.

But the second meeting was held at a different Moose Lodge, so that I could keep everyone separated. Still, the Hells Angels refused to show and the DC Eagles returned without their Boss. Nine other clubs—Low Lyfz, Madmen, Fugarwe Tribe, Wicked Saints, The Brothers, Sokol Riders, Arm, New Attitude, Death Mauraders, Sojourners—also came. At the third meeting I held mock elections, became chairman of the board, and filled the seats of vice chairman, treasurer, and secretary with my closest friends.

And, I nominated the first broad to an official position—Yo

Adrienne who'd serve as corresponding secretary in charge of minutes.

Jaws on his bike

"You can't do that," some Outlaws protested.

"The COC is about equality," I preached. "Just because we wear patches doesn't mean we have to act like assholes."

In time, meetings moved to the South Side clubhouse after the COC's $5,000 donation to Mooseheart went unacknowledged.

My real challenge came when I decided to probate for the Outlaws. I needed an edge—criminal "bona fides" to help me accomplish my goal: control of Chicago. And staying a Loyal Order wasn't going to get me there.

"You don't think that's going to be a conflict?" Jaws asked.

"What's the problem?"

"Aren't you supposed to be neutral?"

"Yeah."

"Don't the Outlaws discriminate against—"

"Compartmentalization," I cut him off. "Acting. I can play two roles."

5

ON THE ISLAND OF MISFIT TOYS

The man at the top of the mountain didn't fall there.

—BIG PETE

Probating reminded me of college and my freshman year, when I pledged the TKE (Tau Kappa Epsilon) fraternity, referred to by some as "an all-male secret society." I solicited so many members that TKE headquarters in Indianapolis invited me to apply to be their national recruiter. Though the fraternal structure held some fascination because it involved calculated manipulation—prospects, sponsors, hazing, loyalty tests, club dues, and brotherhood—I was really more enthralled with organized crime. (In fact, had I not decided to become a gangster, I would most definitely have been a television evangelist. . . . Maybe in the end they're the same thing?)

Greased Lightning sat near the bar, his legs dangling several inches from the floor. Backlash pulled Debbie close, winked at me, and said, "You're a good ol' lady. You make Peter shine."

I could tell Debbie was nervous; she came from corporate America, managed an IT department, rooms and rooms of button-down, pasty-faced men doing the jobs they were trained to do, never asking why, just working, working until the fuzzy white glow above their cubicles dimmed long after the day disappeared. Maybe Debbie felt alive here, in this world that existed Outside: Out (of the) Law, hence Outlaws. Broads in this world had defined roles, scripts, costumes, and understudies. They wore "Property of" vests, filled orders for Bosses and brothers, and stayed mostly marginal, mostly ornamental.

"There's no pressure here to be . . . anything," Debbie said. She found relief in invisibility. "Women need to feel safe," she enlightened me later. "That's it. That's our big secret."

Still, I debated whether to leave the safety of the Loyal Order for the danger of the Outlaws.

"You've always wanted to be a part of something that *mattered*." Debbie insisted the transfer to a "real biker gang" would be a personal challenge for her as well.

"I want this group of misogynists to treat me like a human being, to respect me and refer to me by name. These men who hate women will not hate me. I'll be the best ol' lady the Outlaws have ever seen." She smiled. "My whole purpose will be to make you look good."

That sounded reasonable.

I studied the room of scantily clad broads serving up shot glasses of Crown Royal to drunks at the bar. In a corner, a brother dropped his pants to his ankles and spread his legs wide. A blond head bobbed between them. A skinny broad with hollow eyes danced provocatively on a makeshift stage.

Outlaws whooped and clapped, their laughter resounding like tin in my ears.

I may have been the "new kid in town," but I made sure I would not go unnoticed. I headed to the jukebox, flipped through Southern rock tunes, Lynyrd Skynyrd, Guns N' Roses, AC/DC, the Eagles. I dropped in my coins, and the lyrics resonated. . . .

Where you been lately?

There's a new kid in town. . . .

Johnny come lately, the new kid in town. . . .

And on a dangerously cold January day with a wind-chill warning of thirty degrees below, I threw my card in the hat and became an official probationary member of the Outlaws (aka a probate). I was forty-three, and suddenly a Regional Boss's kid.

But, my lightning-speed alliance with a Regional Boss created dissension in the ranks. Bosses (especially Regional Bosses) did not sponsor recruits. No one needed to know my "fast pass" into the club was cocaine. Further complicating matters was the fact that Greased Lightning was from the South Side chapter and his bodyguard, Backlash, was from Joliet. The Outlaws huddled at "Church" to discuss the conflict. In the end, the regional vice president (who was also from Joliet) informed me, "I'm sending you to Joliet."

As a probate, I expected exhausting weeks of guard duty and errand-boy orders reminiscent of my fraternity days. Instead, my introduction to indentured servitude was the annual Daytona Bike Week at Daytona Beach in Florida. Every

Outlaw was required to attend; the event attracted a mixture of hard-core gangsters, leather-clad professionals, topless "beer girls," aging rebels, and kids on crotch rockets. Bikes and people paraded down Main Street in Daytona Beach. Classic rock blasted into the hot wind.

My first post was guard duty for a row of unattended bikes on a hot, dusty lot. Sun blasted my face. My eyes watered from the brightness. Only two hours in and I already had a raging headache. My legs cramped from standing. Random fingers clicked at me, the sound reverberating hollowly inside my head, too loud, and I suppressed the overwhelming urge to snap the clicker's neck with my bare hands.

"Who's your daddy?" the voice boomed.

His words landed like punches. I wanted to pummel him, react with a hard jab to the throat. He spit, and the glob landed near my boot.

"I'm probating for the Outlaw Nation."

The muscles in his face relaxed. He uncurled his fist. He reeked of alcohol. I knew I had narrowly missed a beating.

"Beer." He shook his hot dog at me. *I wasn't built for speed*. Out of breath and sweaty from effort, I returned with a large, filled paper cup and resumed my post. My lips cracked from sun and dehydration, I heard the call again: "Probate!" Again, I trotted off to fetch the asshole beer. Inside the air-conditioned bar, Outlaw bigwigs drank.

A probate tending bar handed me a foamy mug. He had two black eyes. A welt puffed on the side of his head. Fresh blood oozed from his lip. Blisters formed on his nose. Another probate, being led through the crowd like a tethered cow, recited the name of each brother in the room. But the crowd had swelled to more than fifty.

"What's my name?" an Outlaw in the back of the room shouted at the probate. He hesitated—*punch!* He said the wrong name. *Punch!* He tried again. *Punch!* He threw up. *Punch!*

A chorus started in the back of the bar, "Probate! Probate! Probate!" The bartender slid the mug to me. I knew if he stayed beyond midnight he would likely be human pulp by morning.

When I could no longer feel my legs and my mind had started to take trips to the ocean and I could literally taste salt water sloshing down the back of my throat, I heard, "Peter Pan, come with us."

I expected more torture scenarios, but instead my sponsor ordered me to "stoke the bonfire."

"He's throwing sticks into flames?" Gold Region Boss Milwaukee Jack* lost his mind. He sneered at me. "I ought to take you to Milwaukee, show you what it's *really* like to probate."

"If my dad orders me to go, I'll go."

"Who's your dad?"

I threw out my sponsor's name.

"Regional Bosses are not supposed to have kids." Jack marched off to confront my sponsor. I knew he wouldn't give me up. After all, I supplied him with unlimited cocaine.

Big guys clustered together. My size, for the first time, be-

---

* He would later become the National Boss of the Outlaws MC.

came an asset. Even patched large brothers gave me deference. One even offered me a tip: "When you get off guard duty in twelve hours, take your shoes off." On my breaks I began to air my feet. Heaven. Just that small tip rejuvenated me.

"What's your name?" the voice boomed in my head.

"Probating Outlaw, Chicago, North Side, Pete."

"Peter Pan." He sneered. "What's *my* name?"

Well fuck, I forgot his name. I stood in a crowd of two hundred drunken Outlaws and spent the next hour trying to find out. I felt a little like the baby bird from P. D. Eastman's book *Are You My Mother?*

"I'm JD," one of them said as he smacked me on the side of my head and grinned. I resisted the urge to smash him through the wall. Another patted his chest. "I'm Mother-fucker." I weaved in and out of sweaty bodies, searching for names that made sense that might relieve me from my inane search. But this was a test; they tossed me from brother to brother, mixed up their names, gave me false monikers until the room spun.

"Enough! Get me a screwdriver," a brother said, shoving me toward the bar.

The bartender shook his head. "We're out of orange juice."

I reported back the news.

"So?" The brother shrugged. Off I went to the grocery store to buy orange juice. At least it was a chance to escape the heat.

The year I probated was the last year probates wore identifying markers on the *back* of their vests. Most, who looked at me from the front, dismissed me as a likely club supporter (and not a lowly probate) and left me alone. Still, I had my fair share of slave chores—fetching beer, lighting smokes, and supplying endless condoms and Rolaids to brothers in need. I carried a probate kit with at least three different kinds of toothpaste, toothpicks, tampons (in case someone bled out), rolling paper.

"Peter Pan, got a toothpick?"

I handed him my stash.

"Got a *round* toothpick?"

After that, I mastered disappearing. Big Butch helped.

He always stuffed two Polish sausages in the side pockets of his vest.

"Sometimes I get hungry when I ride," he said with a shrug as wind blew little drops of ketchup down his chin and vest. The sausage wrapper stuck to his windshield.

"We're large," Butch shouted through mouthfuls of onion and meat. "We're good for manual labor."

Big guys had it easier.

Still, no one called me "Big Pete"; instead I was nicknamed "Pete," which sounded a bit like a cartoon character. (Personally, I liked the name "John Wayne," but the serial killer *John Wayne* Gacy sullied the name for me.)

"I really don't like 'Pete.' " I complained to Frank, whose real name was James Lee Wheeler.*

---

* Wheeler, the Outlaws' international president Taco Bowman's successor, was indicted in September 2002 along with thirteen others for racketeering, conspiracy to commit racketeering, and

"Peter James . . ." He thought about it a minute and then smiled. "I'm really Frank James. We used to have a brother in the club named *Jesse* James, but he's dead. You can be my new 'Jesse.' We can be 'Frank and Jesse, the James brothers'— you know like the Younger gang?"

I could see that.

The whole name thing reminded me of my fraternity days, when brothers prophetically called me *King* James.

"Frank likes the big ones." Butch grinned.

"Big ones?"

"Big guys. Like us."

"Big" was a title *and* a definition: "Big Butch"; "Big Mike"; "Big Pete."

In my first month it seemed like every week a brother died. We rode miles to attend the funerals, sometimes two in one day; the cost alone—nearly $100 a person per funeral—was crushing (those chapters who didn't show up were fined). To save money, I bunked in a shit hole with four guys stuffed to a room. We barely showered, slept, or even ate.

We probates were like windup toys, climbing onto our bikes, zipping down expressways, sobering up for the services, barely remembering whose body was inside the casket, before mounting our bikes again and heading to *another* funeral. And another and another until finally the scenery blurred, the cause of death—bike wrecks, diabetes, stabbings,

---

conspiracy to distribute drugs. He is serving sixteen and a half years in prison.

shootings, overdoses—like a multiple choice, was just part of the cost of doing business.

Debbie helped the probates—"but not too much," she assured me. "I never wanted to enable them." She hoped when they were promoted to patched Outlaws, they would remember "Debbie, Big Pete's ol' lady."

She elaborated, "It was important that I earned their respect."

She wanted them to remember she gave them garbage bags to transport trash to the Dumpsters. She cleaned toilets and mopped floors when probates suffered guard duty.

"I did that. And I did a good job."

She wore a T-shirt with a printed message, "Ladies Love Outlaws." Some salivated. But before anyone could paw her or ask her for beer refills, Debbie would replenish their cups or top off their water jugs. She carried extra forks in her pockets, "just in case an Outlaw asked for one, or dropped his, or used several to stab a hamburger off the stovetop."

"It's survival," Debbie said, before sharing with me the mantra seasoned ol' ladies preached: "Make your ol' man look good and no one will mess with you. Be 'Pete's ol' lady, Property of Big Pete.'"

"I feel like I'm back in school," Debbie told everyone.

"I went to school once." Backlash's ol' lady, Gina, giggled.

Debbie brightened, hopeful that maybe she had found some commonality with the broads after all.

"What did you study?"

"Prison."

Debbie had a genuinely pure soul, and I worried she

might not fit in my world, but she felt she "finally belonged somewhere. Being here is what gets me through my life. My job is to serve. Everyone has the same responsibility. It isn't confusing. I'm not weird, and if I can make it here, I can survive anywhere. I just have to remember the Outlaws are real people."

"We're pigs." Poison smacked Debbie's ass. "You're lovely. What's your name?"

"Big Pete Chicago North Side's old lady." She refilled his mug.

"I like you. You're lucky. I might not hurt you."

One night the power shut off in the clubhouse, suddenly, inexplicably, and panic erupted. Lights, air, music, fans—all gone. Glass shattered, screams were muffled, chairs scraped back, toilets flushed. Bodies slammed into me. Some scrambled toward the exits, mowing down brothers in their stampede.

In the pitch darkness, Debbie called out my name. "Pete? Pete?"

The fear in her voice stopped me cold. *This was my wife. This was suddenly real.* I couldn't protect her here. More important, concern for her safety could get *me* killed. This lack of control spun me into a kind of mad-slapped frenzy. But before I could reach her, the room flooded with light again, and with Backlash's maniacal laughter.

He clapped slowly, dramatically in the center of the room. Aftershock surrounded him. Broads shook, sniveled; fat tears wet their cheeks. Brothers scrambled to their feet, crunching on shards of broken glass. A crack split the wall mirror behind the bar. A brother grabbed a rag and dabbed his temple.

Backlash cupped his hands to his mouth and said in an exaggerated announcer's voice, "That was just a drill; I repeat, that was just a drill." More laughter.

Debbie sat on the edge of our couch, visibly shaken. Maybe for the first time, she grasped the Outlaws' dangerous lifestyle. The club wasn't just about partying, and her role in it wasn't just about service. The specter of prison was real.

"Backlash likes to fuck with the probates. The first thing the Feds do when they raid a place is shut off the power." I wasn't very good at being comforting, or protecting her. "I don't think you should come with me to the clubhouse anymore."

She started to cry.

"The only way I can keep you safe is to make sure you know nothing. The Feds will try to get to me through you," I said. "Don't even *whisper* my name."

"But I *want* to help. I serve a purpose."

"Get your tops off," Backlash said as he pounded his fists on the counter the next day. A row of slobbering drunks chimed in, and soon a chorus of "Take it off, take it off" filled the space.

Debbie froze in the melee of peeled T-shirts, ripped bras, and other stray clothing. My chest tightened. I resisted the urge to drag her out of there. She didn't belong in this place, and I realized she was here because of *me,* because I chose to join the Outlaws. And that I couldn't protect her.

The broads writhed to the heavy pulse, kept beat to the

wild claps. Some stripped to G-strings and recklessly buried Outlaws' faces in their crotches.

"You don't have to participate," Backlash's ol' lady told Debbie. "It's your choice. You can decide how you want to be treated. If you want to be a drunk, a slob, a stupid cunt—"

"I want to be Pete's old lady."

"That's a good start." Gina laughed. "We women don't matter anyway."

6

DECONSTRUCTING CHARLIE

You're here to break down doors, not mix drinks.

—BIG BUTCH

Northside Clubhouse Crew. Left Back Row: Maurice, Das Jew, Big Butch, Rabbi, Stones. Front Row: Iron Mike, Bastardo, Big Pete, Chavez, Judas, Blockhead, Pots.

On July 31, exactly six months and one week after I began probating, Frank tossed me an Outlaw top rocker and said, "Hope you know how to sew!"

Cheers erupted from the crowd, followed by "Sew it on, sew it on, sew it on." Shot glasses were raised; I was doused in Crown Royal. My eyes stung. Pride swelled inside me as I waved the top rocker like a flag. Outlaws bear-hugged me, backslapped me, and howled their congratulations. *I had made it! I couldn't fucking believe it. I was an Outlaw, part of a criminal organization.* I grinned so wide my face hurt.

Later, when the pace slowed, Frank gathered everyone in a huddle and said he had something special to read to me.

"He's quite the poet," Butch whispered, leaning on me for balance.

Frank raised his right hand, and I did the same. "Repeat after me," he said, and recited his original Oath.*

"I, Jesse, will show honor, loyalty, and brotherhood." *Repeat.*

"I will never dishonor the Outlaw Nation or all brothers present."

Repeat.

"I will do my best to be a true Outlaw brother; I swear this to the Outlaw Nation and to all brothers present."

Repeat.

I was tipsy, euphoric; the words tumbled out of my

---

* Frank wrote a lot of poetry, including the line, "Riders of the Highway, Brothers 'til the end, Our way of life, The world doesn't comprehend."

mouth. I raised my shot glass again and slammed back another Crown Royal.

"This club will break your heart." Frank's tone sent a
chill down my back.

The following week, Santa and the twenty-two members of
his clean-and-sober club, the New Attitudes, who pros-
pected with me, patched over in one breath, like a one-size-
fits-all, though I had no idea *why* a group that strived to live
"alcohol-and-drug-free" would possibly want to join the
Outlaws. Unless, of course, they were masochists. That fit;
it would sort of be like inviting Alcoholics Anonymous to a
party fully stocked with booze.

"At least they'll have no excuses if they fuck up!" Butch
laughed.

True. Santa's club accepted their patches with measured
enthusiasm, like the last players chosen for flag football. In
time, most gave in to temptation; only seven remained clean
and sober.

"They're like elves." Debbie slid across from Butch and
me on a picnic bench and bit into a cheeseburger. Dusk cast
our faces in shadow. "I don't trust Santa."

"It doesn't matter. I'm only going to use him." I reduced
people to mathematical equations so I could predict their
next move. Santa was an algebra problem (indecisive+
sneaky=untrustworthy=easily manipulated).

Being an Outlaw was about respect.

"You should have seen the boil they lanced off my balls
last week." Butch squeezed a glob of ketchup onto his bun.

Debbie paled mid-chew, and slowly returned her half-eaten burger to her paper plate.

"So much pus on the thing doctors had to bandage it up with a maxi pad."

Debbie left the table.

"Where the fuck are they going?" Butch motioned to Santa and his New Attitudes/Outlaws/Elves.

"We're calling it a night, folks," Santa plastered a smile to his face and waved. "It's getting a little late for us."

Butch stopped chewing, looked at me, his mouth open and full of food, and said, "It's only eight o'clock."

I wanted to make it up to Debbie, involve her in something significant. I surprised her at work.

"What are you doing here?" She smothered a smile and drew me into her suffocating cubicle. Several pushpins stabbed yellow sticky notes to the corkboard wall behind her computer; meeting reminders, to-do lists, appointments, a wedding photo with a Magic Markered black heart outlining our heads. She wore pressed white slacks, a stiff poplin blouse, and wedge heels. Her coworkers gawked: I collected her fully dressed as an Outlaw.

"Thought you could use some fresh air." I grinned.

"I only get an hour for lunch."

"This might take a little longer. Frank needs our help . . . moving water."

"Heard you once owned a soda pop company?" Frank pointed to the rows of skinny bottles with frosted tips stacked on the far wall of the bar. The labels read "Biker Coolant."

"Bottled water?"

"*Biker* water."

He explained his monopoly: Monthly, he sold fifteen to twenty cases of his product, Biker Coolant, to clubhouses and support chapters in and around Chicago, and "made a killing."

As he spoke through his tangled salt-and-pepper beard, I conjured up other saleable products, like bottled oxygen, carbonated "vitamin liquid," and funky clear plastic containers filled with tap water. (This was before Evian, Fiji, and Dasani appeared on the market.)

"Are you in?"

Frank backed his semitrailer into the driveway of the Gary, Indiana clubhouse and unhitched the back flap. In an overgrown, grassy field, high wooden fence posts lined the property like an Old West cavalry.

The crates, stacked in a back barn, resembled moonshine. Debbie climbed onto a pile of old newspapers.

"Don't move from that spot," I said.

"Why aren't you helping?" Frank stacked two crates at her feet.

"My ol' man told me to wait right here."

He looked amused. "Is that right? Who's your ol' man?"

"Big Pete."

"*Jesse!*"

We huddled inside the cab of Frank's semi. Rain started

to fall. Big plops smacked the windshield. Debbie didn't move, not even when rain leaked through slats in the roof and soaked through the newspapers she sat on.

"She's got to help." Frank said. "It's how this works. It's what broads do."

"Of course." I knew that, but I hated to watch as Debbie lifted a crate, struggled a bit with the weight, smiled weakly at me and stepped into the rain. This life claimed casualties.

After several more deliveries, Frank proposed I hit up my COC to buy cases of Biker Coolant, promising me a percentage of the profit. We didn't know each other well, but when the head of the Outlaws asks to partner in business . . . "No" is not an answer. The power Frank yielded was so striking that even a federal judge would later marvel at the "influences of evil one person could have over another."

But when Frank didn't pay up after the first large delivery of Biker Coolant, I debated whether to mention my missing percentage. No chance he simply "forgot" our agreement. If I let the debt go, I would establish a disastrous precedent. Frank might always "forget," and eventually I would be free labor.

"Jesse?"

We sat in the cab after another delivery. A ball formed in the pit of my stomach, my hands clammy on the steering wheel.

"You have a balance due." *It felt so good to get it out.* Like releasing a fart.

Frank raised an eyebrow. He blew out a sigh. I held my breath, not sure what to expect: denial, a punch to the jaw, return to probate status?

He nodded, looked away. "How much?"

I scribbled the figure on a piece of paper and slid it over the dashboard.

"I was wondering if you would have the balls to confront me." He glanced at the number.

I didn't say anything. I actually didn't know what to say. I didn't think of my demand as risky or bold or even stupid. After all, I'd *earned* the percentage. *I was only asking for what was fair.*

"You're a little different than most, aren't you?" Frank laughed.

I was. I really was. In fact, a guy like me only comes along every 150 years.

"I suppose you want the money?"

"It's a substantial figure," I said.

Frank nodded. No apology, no explanation. Instead, he offered to pay up at the National in a week.

I would have to drive my car. There was no way I was going to haul that much money in bills on my bike. We met in an abandoned hothouse with no electricity. Chipped paint peeled off the walls, nails were scattered on the floor, and broken windows gaped open to an alley. Frank handed me a wad of cash. "Want me to count it?"

"Don't insult me."

He grinned. "We're good?"

I tucked the money into my front waistband. "Yeah, we're good."

"You staying?"

"That wouldn't be smart."

We stood in the dark in awkward silence for a few minutes, and then Frank said, "That Joliet chapter—it's a real shit hole."

I shrugged, "Yeah, well . . ."

"I'm heading to Thailand soon, but when I get back you should leave."

"Leave?"

"Get the fuck out of there. Go to Chicago North Side. It only has six members, and Greek, their Boss, needs a complete overhaul."

Frank was either promoting me or hoping to create distance between us, not wanting the whole money issue to become a source of embarrassment or curtail future business dealings.

"Church starts at eight in the morning," Frank said. "Good luck."

But I didn't accept the promotion immediately. Instead I observed (for six months) as treasurer, watching the flow of money in and out of the chapter. I arrived at seven in the morning sharp for Church, to a dark and empty clubhouse. I had a set of keys, and ran my hand along the paint-chipped wall looking for a light switch. Frigid water soaked my boots. A white fuzz bathed the room. Pipes leaked; water stained the ceiling in a yellow-brown circle. A raw-sewage smell lingered in the air. A Confederate flag was draped over the bathroom door. A toilet had overflowed, and I half wondered if I wasn't standing in urine. At eight-fifteen, eight-twenty, eight-thirty, members strolled in, ready for Church.

Some called to let me know they were running late. "What makes you so special that we should all wait for you?"

"Can you believe this shit?" I complained to Debbie. "It's like the 'Home for Wayward Boys.'"

She looked worried.

"A chapter is a *business*," I said the following week at Church. The six members had all shown up, but some of them had fallen asleep.

"A house has to be self-sufficient. Club dues can't go to pay for this shit." I pointed to the cracked concrete walls and exposed electrical cords. I proposed a plan: "If each chapter pays a hundred dollars a month, the chapter is going to *lose* money. We need to charge twenty-five dollars *weekly*. With fifty-two weeks in the year, that's an extra hundred dollars a year."

Some noticed the subtle change: I eliminated all balances, started the chapter at zero, and required all officers to pay dues.

"You're good at this," Greek said as he rode with me to Church one morning. "We actually have more money than we've ever had."

"Maybe *you* should run for Boss," a brother said as he pulled me aside one night.

"Elections" are always over before they even happen. I agreed to "run" for the position of Boss, but only after I first informed Greek.

"Would it be okay if I nominated you?" Greek stared at his hands. "You know I never wanted to be Boss in the first place. Do you have a plan to fix this mess?"

"We're going to go back to having fun," I said. "And no one better be late."

Or there would be consequences: $100 fines, black eyes, a probate vest.

But loyal recruits proved to be difficult to find: Being a one-percenter wasn't a title, it was a lifestyle, a weird rescue from the mundane. Most recruits were either gangbangers (the good ones were either dead or in prison by the time they were thirty-five) or "ham-and-eggers"—unskilled and uneducated, with no social or economic credentials beyond a colorful criminal record.

I subjected probates to tests:

"We need eight-ounce plastic cups for the party." Black Head led the charge. He scurried off to fulfill the order and returned with a plastic bag filled with sixteen-ounce cups.

"That's not what I ordered." I shook my head. "*These* are going to *cost* the chapter money."

Black Head didn't understand.

"If you pour beer into sixteen-ounce cups you're going to lose some profit." I slowed down my words and tried again with another brother, Brutal. "We need A&W Root Beer for the party."

He returned with *Mug* Root Beer. Now I was really pissed off.

"What's the big deal?" Brutal asked.

"The big *deal*"—my whole body tensed—"is that I *asked* for A&W. If you can't follow simple directions . . ."

I held meetings about following directions and arranged

meetings about meetings and organized committees to supervise the meetings.

"I'm telling you, it's like *Who's On First,* " I confided to Debbie later.

Two months after I became Boss, my Regional Boss presented Debbie with her "Property of" vest. Most ol' ladies received theirs in six months or more, but Debbie earned hers early and, though the production was unceremonious, it elevated her status; she was now part of a family, not just a civilian playing dress-up.

"Anyone can wear a wedding ring; not anyone can get a Property vest," she said as she modeled for the ol' ladies.

"I couldn't do it. I'd be too paranoid." One passaround shook her head. "Always on the lookout for violence, Feds, crime. You're a moving target."

"You're an important person's wife now." Gina laughed.

With that came responsibility and a few do's and don'ts:

The property vest is not a costume;
The Feds know all;
Assume you are under surveillance;
Watch the rearview mirror;
Study people as if they will harm you;
And, if you suspect you're being followed, drive in a
     circle—make three right turns,
and if by the third right the car is still there, get the
     license plate and lose the tail.

I taught her other things, too, simple commonsense things, like never leave the porch light on at night.

"That just signals I'm not home," I told her. "Turn it on *during* the day and it will confuse people."

"And steer clear of vans that have their windows rolled down. Chances are there are guns pointing out."

She carried a knife.

7

WISEGUYS

I was like a musician: I crossed all genres . . .

—BIG PETE

The Outlaws shared a symbiotic relationship with the Chicago Outfit (aka "Mafia"). Both organizations operated as shadow governments controlling legitimate businesses in completely unlawful ways and commanding an army of psychopathic killers. Both syndicates trained soldiers and bosses to single-mindedly focus—twenty-four hours a day, seven days a week—on "how to make money for the Family." The oath was a lifetime contract; betrayal resulted in death (or prison, and *then* death). Any crime had to be cleared first through the Outfit.* The Chicago Heights and Cicero crews used the Outlaws mostly to do

---

* Unlike New York's infamous Five Families, the Chicago mob consists of only one family, called "the Outfit." It is organized into a variety of "crews" that engage in criminal activity.

their thug work, but there were also "earners"* among them. Like *me*.

"How about we put video gambling machines in all the clubhouses?" Chef Corleone said as he slid across from me one day, cigar in mouth. He dressed well[†]: silk gray slacks, shiny shoes, nice little shirt, moderate jewelry. I had a table off the bar at the Capri, Chef's "fine dining" establishment in upscale Melrose Park.

This exchange occurred in 1995, and the Outlaws already had a reputation as warmongers and murderous rogues known to detonate whole blocks of buildings, "virtually disintegrate" parked cars, gun down rival gangsters, and critically maim curious citizens.

The battles for enemy turf involved street rumbles, fistfights, stabbings, shoot-outs, and bombings. At first, the wars were private affairs, club business handled in dark places away from public scrutiny. But the bombings of 1995, the "bang, bang, bang" that sounded at first like backfire from a Harley-Davidson, signaled the start of something gone "deeply awry in the underground world of motorcycle gangs."

We were officially at war with the Hells Angels and their club supporters.

Chef tapped his thick finger on the table. "Think about it." *I had taken a giant pay cut to become an Outlaw, and*

---

* A higher associate
† "Biker War Erupts in Illinois" by Jerry Thomas, Chicago Tribune, November 20, 1994

wasn't wild about sharing profits. If I was going to do this gambling thing, it was going to be a solo act, on my terms.

Back in the day, when the Feds arrested loan sharks, book-makers, and small-time operators running illegal card and dice games, their sentences were suspended or they did jail time of a year or so at most. The Racketeer Influenced and Corrupt Organizations Act (RICO) and Title III electronic surveillance provisions implemented in the 1970s dramatically changed this.

RICO was aimed at a systematic pattern of criminal activity. If any two criminal acts—murder, extortion, loan-sharking, and so on—could be linked to a particular family or organization, it allowed the government (in theory) to target members as a criminal enterprise, with far more severe penalties.

Mr. Happy, a self-prescribed "fence" for the Chicago Outfit's Cicero crew, invited me one day to "check out his shop," after first saying, "Heard you're putting machines in your clubhouses."

"I haven't decided anything yet."

The Feds weren't interested in run-of-the-mill gambling cases. They wanted the top guys, the movers and shakers.

Still, several days later, I accepted Mr. Happy's invitation to visit his cramped "pawnshop" (aka Goldberg Jewelers) in Cicero, an area a federal judge once dubbed the "epicenter of organized crime." Mr. Happy sold "a little piece of every-thing": cigarettes, electronics, and various goods from robberies of jewelry stores and homes committed by the criminal enterprise operating in and around Cicero.

Behind bulletproof glass, Mr. Happy placed scales to measure precious jewels, acid trays to test gold, machines to remove serial numbers from shotguns and grenades. The Outfit owned the adjacent empty building and stocked it full with piles of cash. It was the same nondescript building I had stared at as a kid when my uncle rented a room across the street at the Shamrock Inn, a three-story motel famous for card games.

After partying all night, I dragged myself into Mr. Happy's "pawnshop" through the back gate, dressed in sweatpants and baggy shirt, my hair tangled. I stank of smoke. Wiseguys milled around me, studying me cautiously as Mr. Happy prattled on about the Outfit's "interests" in loan-sharking, gambling, pornography, liquor service to restaurants and nightclubs, and produce and meat wholesale distribution.

"Some business deals," he cautioned, "required La Cosa Nostra's (LCN's)* approval."

"You sweep the place, right?"

I became increasingly uneasy with his banter. The government had bugs, zoom lenses, video cameras, surveillance equipment. *And right now, given how disheveled and wasted I was, I probably looked like a psychopathic killer.*

---

* While New York typically received most of the attention for LCN, Al Capone and the Chicago LCN were also players. Over time the crews blended into legitimate businesses and unions— cold-blooded murder attracted unwanted attention from law enforcement.

"It's fucking alarmed." Mr. Happy waved me over to a window and pulled out a pair of binoculars. "Check this out." He zeroed in on a white van parked across the street.

"The Feds sit out there because they can't get in here," he said.

"Who are you talking to about machines?" Chef asked me the next week.

Now I was really pissed. "Look, I haven't agreed to do this."

Two days later, I visited Mr. Happy's shop again, saying I was in the market for rings. (I purchased a grenade ashtray instead.) A line formed behind the bulletproof glass. A man wrapped in rags tried to sell tools he'd probably stolen from a repair truck.

Mr. Happy nodded. "Yeah, okay." But before he showed me his inventory, he insisted "some guy" wanted to meet me.

"What guy?"

Mr. Happy glanced at his watch.

The room grew suddenly quiet, too quiet. My exit shrunk to a small slit in the concrete. My head clouded, the way it did when my claustrophobia took hold.

"He'll be here in five minutes."

"The Large Guy" appeared in the doorway, backlit by street globes, looking every bit a mobster; pinstripes, chunky cuff links, felt flat cap, and leather gloves. He was wide like me, with fire-tipped hair, a clean-shaven chin, and droopy brown eyes. I expected to "walk and talk"—take mindless trips around the block, up and down alleys, left turns, sharp rights, past the Feds' white van with its windows zipped down, recording every hushed tone.

But instead, we spoke freely in the back room, surrounded by stacks of crates.

"Things happen a certain way around here," the Large Guy began. "Chef . . . He's just a cook, you know?"

Yeah okay.

My paranoia increased. Clusters of precious jewels lay exposed in a basket in the front entrance of my home so thieves would have something quick to snatch. At parties I ordered random strip searches, because wands and transmitters could only detect wires that were actually switched *on*. I worried about phones and never answered unknown numbers (the calls were either from telemarketers or Feds). I never answered doorbells, either (probably delivery guys—the kind that wore explosives).

"Are you sure it's safe to talk in here?" I asked Mr. Happy again and again.

I consulted Audrey, a tarot reader a few blocks from my home.

"I'm worried people are talking about me," I told her.

Audrey flipped over the hourglass and closed her blue-eye-shadowed lids. Loose curls draped her shoulders. Her body disappeared inside a flowery tent dress as she shuffled cards and formed three even piles on the table.

"Left, middle, or right," she took my hands in hers and whispered a prayer.

"Middle," I said.

She spread the cards in a Celtic cross and flipped over the Devil and Fool.

"That can't be good," I said.

"Take an empty mayonnaise jar." She stared at me intently. "Write the person's name in white crayon on black crepe paper and put it into the jar and fill it with water."

Later that night I did exactly as Audrey instructed. I placed the jar on the windowsill and watched the paper turn to paste.

"What's with the empty mayonnaise jar?" Debbie asked.

"Jessica wants me to meet her new boyfriend."

"And you put a spell on him?"

I probably *should* have. My daughter so rarely asked me to play Father. . . .

I wanted to bring her something, a token of my gratitude, but what gift would a daughter want from a father who was mostly absent?

"Thanks." Jessica looked a little puzzled as I slid a small television across the restaurant table. I resisted the urge to tell her she could choose anything she wanted from an entire warehouse of electrical goods. She had her mother's olive complexion. Sparkly hoop earrings dangled to her shoulders; she wore a plain white blouse and sensible wedge shoes.

The boyfriend looked ready to bolt as he sat on the edge of a cracked foam cushion and ordered coffee. Tall and thin, with a whip ponytail down the small of his back, he extended a sweaty hand.

"Good to meet you." The veins in his arms formed little blue rivers beneath his skin.

"What do you do for a living?"

Jessica stared at the menu.

The boyfriend stuttered, "What do you mean?"

"Am I speaking English?"

Jessica glared at me.

I realize my question was a little hypocritical considering *I* had no real job, but this was my daughter. . . .

"I'm in between work right now."

I fixated on the creases in the boyfriend's face, his dull, empty eyes, like small rooms with no heat. My hands clenched and unclenched under the table. Current rushed through my body. The whole right side of my face tingled.

"You turned into a version of the Incredible Hulk, didn't you?" Debbie looked at my swollen knuckles. "Just can't control your temper, can you?"

"I couldn't help it."

"It's like a creature bursts through your skin and just takes over."

"He aspired to do nothing, never pay rent, and suck the living shit out of my daughter."

"How bad did you hurt him?" Debbie folded her arms across her chest.

"I don't *think* he went to the hospital." The beating had

been a reflex. I'd yanked him across the table by his ponytail and slammed his perfect nose into the wall.

"Let me make it up to you," I proposed to Jessica later. "I'll take you shopping."

"*Shopping?*"

I took my cue from Mr. Happy, and designed my own "Sam's Club," filled wall to wall with appliances, electronics, computers, radios, phones, designer jeans, even steak and lobster. I never actually "bought" any of the items; they were all "gifts." Hence, Pete's Rule #5: Never do anything for which you cannot afford to pay your lawyer a retainer.

"Pick anything you like," I said.

"Did you *steal* this stuff?" She'd brought her friends.

I ignored her question, just happy to spend time with my daughter, happy she'd dumped the boyfriend, and happy I could be some kind of father to her.

8
ROCK STAR

Pete, Bastardo as a Black Piston, Mr. Happy riding the strip at
Daytona Beach for Bike Week

Financially, life was unpredictable. One week I'd be rolling
in dough, two weeks later dead broke. I never saved any

money. My safety net was another score. When I needed cash, I bought debts and maneuvered the trucks that cleaned out houses for the Outfit.

"Sorry, man, just doing business." I felt a little bad as stunned home owners watched whole furniture sets disappear.

But being Boss required a certain style. Perception was reality—gold wristbands, Rolex watches, jeweled medallions, bracelets, and even a gold finger on my vest above the AOA patch where the swastika used to display.

"I don't imagine they make too many of *those*," a cop remarked once.

"Just one." *It had been a Christmas gift from the brothers and affirmation that they appreciated me.*

"What are you, some kind of rock star?"

I played one.

I traveled first class to Daytona—twenty-two hours, eleven hundred miles, in a truck that hauled three trailers packed full with bikes. Mr. Happy, pumped on Red Bull, drove straight through, stopping only to gas up and piss. Once, a cargo of chickens spilled on the interstate in front of us; Mr. Happy swerved to miss the birds, but clipped several, sending plumes of feathers into the air. Clusters of bloody webbed feet stuck to the windshield. By the time we arrived at the beach, Debbie was green.

"Where you staying?" Ho Jo, an Outlaw from the Red Region, asked when he called a few hours before we arrived. We had met several times before at other biker functions. He was weirdly affable, a stunted, slower, shorter version of me. We bonded almost instantly. Maybe that's just what happens when you encounter yourself.

I'd rented a suite in a five-star hotel overlooking the ocean, while others were going to cram several to a room and stumble over tiny, rumpled beds.

I recited the address to him.

An hour later, Ho Jo called again, whining a little like Joe Pesci. "*Where* are you guys staying?"

"We're here," I said.

"No you're not."

"I'm standing in the hotel." The lobby was crowded with Outlaws.

"No you're not."

My blood pressure spiked. Debbie chuckled. "He's lost, isn't he?"

"No I'm not," Ho Jo yelled.

A bellhop unloaded twenty-five black duffel bags.

"You must be Big Pete," someone said, trying to shake my hand.

"Who the fuck are you?" I didn't recognize his colors. His and his buddy's three-piece patch designs were similar to those of the Unknown Few (not to be confused with another motorcycle club called the Chosen Few or the Insane Unknowns or Just Us Few), only smaller and darker. Same black and white colors, ape handlebars, and a dwarf-sized grinning skull with rotted teeth.

"We're with Ho Jo." He seemed totally lost, unsure whether to retract his outstretched hand or leave it suspended in midair like an awkward extension of his body.

"Ho Jo's not here," I said.

"He's at another hotel with the same name," Mr. Happy said, lowering his voice and stooping to grab my bags.

"What are you, my fucking valet?" I snapped at Mr. Happy.

"We're his support club," the misfit tried again.

"Never heard of you." Though he hadn't yet supplied the name.

"But . . ."

"How many are you?" I only saw two.

Numbers separated the "serious clubs" from the posers. If a new club approached me with fewer than five members, I knew it wouldn't survive a year; most dissolved after a week. Start-ups had to design their patches, ensuring the colors didn't conflict or resemble an existing club's. They had to draft an original constitution, prepare bylaws and mission statements, and recruit prospective followers willing to embrace a certain lifestyle just for the privilege of hanging around a one-percenter.

"That's none of your business," the misfit said.

Mr. Happy prepared to block my blow; he must have registered the subtle change in my expression from irritation to rage. "You're wearing a 'Support Your Local Outlaw' insignia. That *entitles* me to know how many members you have."

"We can't tell you," Misfit's buddy said. He resembled a potato: lumpy hips, bruised skin with patches of brown spots, bald skull, and flaps of excess chin. His T-shirt was practically a tablecloth.

"Who the fuck do you think you are? You're both banished to your rooms for two days. And you are forbidden from talking to any Outlaws."

I could tell they thought I was kidding—"banished" sounded so medieval. But after a dead silence, the two slunk off, dragging their twenty-five bags behind them. Mr. Happy smothered a smile. Debbie smirked.

All I wanted was sleep. The little concierge gave me the card key and said, "I trust everything will meet your expectations." I headed down the hall, so tired my legs barely registered the floor. But when I opened my suite, I saw unmade beds and bunched sheets, and what looked like a naked foot.

"The fuckers didn't even clean first." I fumbled for the light switch.

"Don't kill us!" A blur of white sheets and pink light bulbs flashed across the room. A male voice swore as his big toe smashed into the coffee table.

"Harrryyy!" A broad screamed. "What *is* he?"

"Here's my wallet." The man practically threw it at me. Coins littered the floor. His hands shot into the air. "Don't shoot!"

"What the fuck is going on?"

"Why are there people here?" Debbie gasped.

"I'm not doing this again." I slapped the key card on the concierge's counter. "*You* walk into the next room."

"I'm so sorry, sir, wrong key."

"I'd rather be shot at than labeled a Peeping Tom, for fuck's sake. I'm an Outlaw, you know; I'm with the Outlaws.

Find one of *their* rooms—at least if you open the wrong one, I'll still be with *me*."

Ho Jo stumbled into the lobby. He came up to my waist.

"Hey, Pete, Pete, I'm here." Sweat moistened his forehead.

"Glad you found the place. I met your friends. They're lovely. I sent them to their rooms."

Ho Jo looked confused. "They're with me, you know."

"They misbehaved."

I followed the concierge down the hall. Ho Jo tried to keep up, tripped, trotted along, tripped again.

"Pick him up, will you?" I ordered Mr. Happy, who didn't miss a beat. He scooped up Ho Jo by the armpits and floated him down the hall.

"You have to let them out. . . ." Ho Jo whined.

"I don't *have* to do anything."

The concierge opened my suite. It smelled like ocean.

"How long then?"

"Tell you what." I smiled at the bottle of wine and the two glasses on the balcony. "I'll let one out in a couple days."

Ho Jo called an official meeting at the tiki bar the next afternoon, said he had "serious business" to discuss concerning a growing Outlaw chapter in his Red Region. Several Bosses and I gathered around picnic tables pushed together on a wooden deck. We stirred piña coladas with pretty umbrella straws. The sun warmed our cheeks. A high tide crashed against nearby boulders. The burning tiki torches smelled like French fries.

Ho Jo adjusted his oversized lenses, his short, stubby legs skimming the sand.

I sucked the paper from my straw, my mind wandering to spitballs. I shut my eyes behind my Ray-Bans, letting Ho Jo's voice lull me into a half sleep. He sounded like Morris "Moe" Greene, the character in Mario Puzo's *The Godfather*. Based on Bugsy Siegel, Greene worked as a mobster hit man for the Corleone family and later became a casino proprietor. He received "a Moe Greene special" when an unknown assassin surprised him one day and shot him through the eye.

The wrapper formed a small ball in my mouth, and the more Ho Jo spoke, the more vigorously I soaked the paper with my spit. *I was almost ready.* I cracked open one eye. Bright sun beat against the lid. Ho Jo droned on; the others at the table politely drained their piña coladas, then ordered seconds from the waitress in the red bikini and stiletto heels.

I focused on making the perfect spitball as little beads of sweat slipped behind Ho Jo's lenses.

I paid no attention to his words. Something about "voting" and "rules" and sham "elections." Part of me wanted to interrupt and say, "No one seriously *votes* for anything in this club, do they? It's just critical to let them *think* they're voting." Ho Jo asked for a show of hands. *Was he serious?*

Aim, steady, fire.

The spitball struck like a dart, hitting Ho Jo full on in the left eye before settling on the inside of his giant lens. The effect was pure comedy. He stopped mid-sentence, his hand in the air. He shook his head, probably hoping to dislodge the wet ball. The Bosses at the table had their hands raised too. They looked a little startled.

"You've been Moe-Greened," I roared. And just then the waitress returned with the pretty drinks. The Bosses dissolved into laughter, dropping their hands, pointing, some barely able to catch their breath. The waitress smiled.

"I love you too, brother." Ho Jo whipped off his glasses. I could tell I had embarrassed him. He was conducting a "serious vote" about something "serious," and I had turned his meeting into a mockery. *This was bad. This was really bad.*

Then it happened: payback. Ho Jo wiping his glasses with an edge of T-shirt, me stirring my frozen drink and thinking about an apology, and the waitress jiggling her tits as she slid the drinks across the table, and . . . *plop!* A lone seagull flying above me had shit on my head.

"Now we're even." Ho Jo smirked.

"Tell you what." I didn't bother wiping the poo off my head. "I'll release your captives." Ho Jo brightened. I reached into my jeans pocket and threw a set of keys on the table. "And I'll give you these—they open the North Side clubhouse. You're welcome anytime."

"You can be a real asshole sometimes." Ho Jo grinned.

"Only *part* of the time."

9

WE, THE PEOPLE

I was invited to speak at NCOM's next patch-holders meeting. Twenty-eight chapter chairmen were to gather in the Great Hall to recite their clubs' accomplishments: arranging for stop signs on busy roadways, addressing profiling issues and a "handlebar bill," adopting lane-share options for motorcyclists. *Mundane. Mundane. Mundane.* My goal for NCOM was unification and education, not street improvement projects that made it easier for motorcyclists to navigate the square world. NCOM wasn't about "Us and Them," it was about "Us."

"What will you speak about?" Debbie asked.

I had no idea yet, but "The Omega Glory," a *Star Trek* episode, had been rerun on television the night before. Captain Kirk found Captain Tracey of the USS *Exeter* violating the Prime Directive and interfering with a war between the Yangs and the Kohms (which Kirk concluded finally were just euphemisms for Yankees and Communists, though that seemed a far-fetched story line). *Us and Them.* Captain

Tracey's phrase, "E Plebnista," a bastardized version of "We, the People," replayed in my head as I stood at the podium and stared into the expectant crowd.

"*We* the people," I borrowed from Kirk's speech. "They're the most important three words in the English language. We are *the* people, not *some* people, or sometimes *even* people. We are people. We're not fighting for *road* equality. There is no *Us* and *Them*, there's just us—we the people, one united front."

Applause.

"These are not holy words." Kirk echoed in my head. "They do not just apply to the squares—they must apply to everyone or no one at all."

More applause.

There was no chance anyone else had seen the rerun or the cheesy trailer . . . I hoped.

"We are the people who let this shit happen to us."

The crowd went nuts.

And the *Starship Enterprise* shot into the galaxy, leaving the Yangs to contemplate the meaning of liberty and justice for *all*. . . .

"Hey, Boss, there's this club that wants to remain neutral," the Outlaw named Rider reported to Frank later that week.

"Neutral?"

"That's what they said."

"There's no such thing. They're either with us or against us." Frank swiveled on his bar stool.

"They insist they're independent."

NCOM patch-holders meeting

"They rejected the Angels too?"

"They want to be neutral."

He continued to spin. "All right, fuck 'em, let them try solo, see what happens.

The Odeum* Swap Meet happened. The large-scale event organized in Chicagoland represented the first in Outlaw history the club did not control. Translation: *school*. Outlaws customarily contacted the owner for a "meeting of the minds." It was important everyone understood the "rules": No Angels allowed. If any slipped through, "there might be

---

* Odeum Expo Center in Villa Park, Illinois

bloodshed." The owner listened politely to our demands and then hung up on us. This left us convinced the swap meet was an "Angel" show.

"We'll set up a perimeter," Backlash said, launching into attack mode.

He suggested we prepare the Outlaws' fortified war wagon—an armor-plated van with a gun port, equipped inside with handguns, rifles, a submachine gun, bulletproof vests, smoke grenades, ammunition, and walkie-talkies.

"We'll circle the venue in case things get shitty."

But Joker, the recently named new Regional Boss, vetoed Backlash's idea, thinking it "excessive" and "hardly necessary." He had his own "attack plan," one he had used "quite successfully" when he was a member of the High Spirits, a small "ma and pa" club comprised at the most of ten members. Joker lacked experience; he was no wartime Boss, but he was trying to put up a good front.

"We're going to march inside as a united front, and arrive at the same time," he announced.

"At the same time as what?" I wasn't being an asshole; I really didn't get it.

"The Angels—you know, so they'll know we're there."

"Then what?" I tried to envision his plan: Outlaws and Angels charging the same field at the same time and just flailing about, weapons drawn, each hoping for victory.

"We'll all arrive together," Joker "clarified."

"Sounds like Massacre 101."

Whatever happened to basic military arrangement: infantry in the center, cavalry on the wings, adequate reserves?

Even standard Roman legionnaires' maneuvers included tactics like the Tortoise, shell-like armor soldiers used to shield against incoming arrows (or, in this case, bullets); the Wedge, the short knife useful in hand-to-hand combat; the Saw, an army's response to the Wedge; the Skirmishing formation, a widely spaced line up of troops that allowed for greater mobility; the Repel Cavalry, first, second, and third rank walls of soldiers with their shields and spears drawn, poised for assault as each wall fell; and finally the Orb, a defensive position in the shape of a circle in case all other methods failed.

We relented and followed Joker into battle. The day the swap meet opened, security stopped everyone at the entrance and confiscated knives, pistols, and ammunition.

"He says we can purchase these inside at the booths," Santa shouted as I rode up.

"What are you doing?" I dismounted my bike. The line snaked into the street. Hot sun beat down on citizens and support clubs. Some pushed empty shopping carts, hoping to fill them with merchandise; others had backpacks.

"We're waiting to get in." Santa motioned to his entourage. They were all shorter than him by inches.

"Get out of line," I said. Santa flinched as if I had just slapped him. "We're Outlaws, for fuck's sake."

Santa hesitated, then gave up his place in line. He and his little people trotted behind me toward the gate.

"Let us in," I barked to the guard. "We're Outlaws."

"Enjoy yourselves," the man said with a nod, and ushered us inside the three-story building.

We started on the ground floor, casually observing the

vendor booths, the merchants hawking leathers, T-shirts, sunglasses, used items, toys, kitchenware, jewelry, guns, knives, bows, arrows. I spotted several Hells Angels booths. When I got to five I stopped counting.

"Do you see what I see?" I whispered to Backlash.

"They set up the night before."

"Plenty of time to haul in their Tupperware containers full of T-shirts and modified AR-15 rifles."

Backlash nodded, and blew a small bubble with his gum. "They easily bypassed security." Our mistake was not having purchased booths.

The Angels no doubt had an arsenal hidden in plastic containers that included switchblades, pen guns with silencers, tomahawks, and swords. Backlash pretended to trip on a hanging cloth from an Angel's booth. The booth wobbled, knocking over a few propped items. The broad setting up merchandise glared at him.

"What the fuck are you doing?" Joker yanked him away.

"Being Backlash." He saluted the broad and dramatically stumbled away.

"You want to get us killed?"

His recklessness was a prelude to Joker's "Massacre 101." We were unarmed and clearly surrounded by Angels. Outlaws promptly lined up in droves to purchase folding knives. The swap meet had triple-wide ramps twenty feet long leading to the second and third floors.

"Look who's here." Frank nodded toward the three "neutral" club members who had approached him the week before. They were dressed in muted brown with leather skullcaps and bandannas. Their patch was a mountain peak with a goat, reminiscent of the Swiss Alps.

The scene on the ramp unfolded like something out of a street rumble. The three neutrals were amateurs, lingering too long on the ramp, seemingly oblivious to the Angels who'd drifted near them, moving slowly at first, outnumbering Switzerland by five members. And just when the two groups intersected on a shadowy portion of the platform, the Angels attacked.

"I heard *click, click, click*. Blades extending. I was never so scared in my life. It happened so quickly. They circled the men, stabbed them in the knees, sides, shoulders and just left them bleeding out," one support club member who slithered by the attackers reported.

Ambulances arrived, cops swarmed in, security blew whistles. The three neutrals were strapped to gurneys and carted out.

"What happened here?" A cop stared at me, hands on hips. He didn't bother with a clipboard or pen. He already knew the answer. No one saw anything.

The next day, Super Bowl Sunday, a group of us watched the game at the North Side clubhouse. We were in "recovery mode" from the swap meet debacle. At halftime, we heard a knock at the front door.

"Boss, someone's here to see you."

"The game's on." I didn't move.

"They said they're from the neutral club or some shit."

I put down the remote, went to the door. "Can I help you?"

The neutrals looked worn out, still a little shaken from the day before. One guy's Swiss Alp had a few blood drops on the goat. They didn't bother with skullcaps. Their mascot shifted his weight on his crutches, his right leg bandaged. "We thought it over and . . . we want to join the Outlaws now."

I slammed the door in his face.

10

NEUTRAL GROUND

"Look, this is Chicago—you're an uninvited guest." I cradled the phone to my ear, only half listening to the violator's stutter on the other end. I had two baskets on my desk, one for "Problems Handled" and the other for more drastic measures: "The Brown Van."

"It's Stitch." I slid my slip of paper into Basket #2.

He was a member of Blitzkrieg, a white supremacist club that boasted a shine Boss and a patch embroidered with a Confederate flag and a Nazi-inspired Iron Cross. I first spotted Stitch at an ABATE* picnic the week before.

"He's here."

Without another word, Mr. Happy dragged him over. Stitch wore a wide-brimmed cowboy hat and sunglasses and sneakers with the tongue flipped out. He grinned and sipped

---

* A nonprofit motorcycle rights organization dedicated to freedom of the road for all motorcyclists.

his beer. I punched him hard in the solar plexus. He doubled over, spit up his drink, and dropped to his knees. I kicked him in the mouth, split open his upper lip. I yanked his braid, grabbed his ear, said "Get the fuck up."

Mountain from the South Side joined in. His voice sounded like a stuck car horn. "We will *kill* you. We will kill your fucking family and their fucking kids. We will fuck you up." Spit flew from his mouth.

"Shut up, I got this." I shoved Mountain aside.

"We will fuck you up," he continued.

The picnic abruptly ended—conversations stopped mid-sentence, burgers sizzled and charred on the grill, paper plates and cups were scattered across the grass.

Stitch moaned something about "neutral ground."

"There's no such thing. If I see you again I will cut off your ear."

"I got this." Bastardo nodded to the folded note in Basket #2.

Even so, I felt compelled to instruct him, "Buy the van at auction. Pay no more than two thousand dollars. Make sure it can travel at least the speed limit and has two working back doors."

I planned to recycle the van later into scrap and recoup a small profit from the parts. I wasted nothing, taking my cue from the Outfit, who sometimes chopped up bodies and disposed of the remains as fertilizer. And just in case there were witnesses, I ordered Bastardo to switch out plates with similar stolen ones so that VINs never matched and nothing was ever traceable.

It was critical no one saw me give the orders to inflict harm. "Never *kill*, just badly injure." I suggested spiked bats and stressed, "No Outlaw insignia."

"In and out, crack a few skulls, get back in the van." I didn't want details.

Bastardo gave me updates in code as he completed the job saying things like, "The cheeseburger was outstanding. I'm stuffed."

I put a large "X" through the note and moved it into Basket #1.

The next week several members from the Latin American Motorcycle Association (aka "L.A.M.A.") rolled into the Illinois Harley-Davidson dealership. I pulled up on my bike with Jimmy and left the engine running. "You guys can't be here." I wasn't a complete asshole, believed in due process. This was their warning. A L.A.M.A. member looked a little startled by my boldness, slid his vest aside, and exposed his Glock.

"Careful, I'm a Chicago cop."

"I'm an Outlaw." I didn't flinch.

The cop/Latino/associate blinked and repeated louder, "Maybe you didn't hear me the first time. I'm a *cop*."

"You're not in uniform." I flashed the .38 inside my vest. "That makes you no different than us." I knew he wouldn't shoot. He needed me, needed the Outlaws—we kept the neighborhoods safe. The cop's hands trembled. His face glistened. He chewed his lower lip, caught in that moral snare between being a law enforcer and simply *being* the law. His predecessors had likely faced the same dilemma when they shared spit with the Outfit.

The other L.A.M.A. brothers looked away, pretended to study the shiny chrome on the Harleys displayed in the parking lot. They huddled, debated their next move.

"You think you're the only one here with a gun?" I nodded to Jimmy, who grinned and pulled his pistol.

The L.A.M.A. cop swallowed, stared dully at both barrels, his finger still on the trigger.

"Go on, shoot. There are two of us. You won't survive the second bullet."

He hesitated, and I could tell he was thinking hard about his options. "Should I, shouldn't I" knocked around his skull, until finally he chose humiliation . . . and survival.

Illinois Harley held an open house a month later. I roared into the dealership with fifteen Outlaws. I couldn't believe it. "They're here *again.*"

The L.A.M.A. cop had returned with eight of his associates, each of whom had likely signed a waiver to belong, agreeing to "participate voluntarily and at their own risk in all L.A.M.A. activities and assume all risk of injury and damage arising out of the conduct of such activities."

"Get them out of here," I ordered Mr. Happy.

"They're invited guests," Bob, the owner of the dealership, protested. He had a face like raw meat: sweaty, red, cleaved.

"Is that so?" I said.

"This is neutral ground."

"This is Chicago," I corrected him.

"Come on now."

"How would you like your guests to go home in a box?"

Bob blew out a sigh. "I'm not comfortable with that."

"Would you feel more comfortable if they went to the hospital?"

"We're a family," one L.A.M.A. brother said. "We don't want any trouble."

"You're here." I shrugged.

"We don't tolerate violence," another L.A.M.A. brother volunteered.

Bob looked like he might throw up.

"Who's being violent?" I said.

"We're leaving." The L.A.M.A. cop motioned for his associates to mount their bikes.

"I know." I watched them fishtail toward the interstate.

And the next morning, I placed L.A.M.A. Bob into Basket #2.

"Send the Brown Van." I never had to say much to Bastardo. We spoke a secret language.

"Hey there" meant he had completed the task.

"Angels on the move, be fucking careful" was code for the Brown Van has been dispatched and bloodshed will follow.

And while Bastardo and his crew handled the problem in Basket #2, I unwound at a bar with the Hound. We hid at a back table, hoping to blend into the dirty-wallpaper poppy fields.

"I know who you are." A skinny broad with hollow eyes

stared at me most of the evening. She reminded me of an old stripper, with tattoos in all the wrong places, milk white curls, a few puffy scars. The Hound and I nursed our drinks.

"No you don't."

"I do, I really do." She narrowed her eyes, bummed a cigarette off a patron and held it between her painted fingers.

"She hates you." The Hound laughed.

"I fucking do."

Fighting words. If she had been a man I would have coldcocked her right there, but instead I listened, amused, and reviewed in my head the possible dangerous ways we knew each other.

"You're mean. And there's not one redeeming quality about you." She jammed the unlit butt into the counter, grabbed her sparkly purse, and left.

"Well then." The Hound tapped his beer to my glass. "I think that says it all."

Just the *thought* of violence drained me. "I think I'll head home." I slipped a few bills for a tip under my empty glass of Crown Royal.

"Good idea—counterbalance."

"What do you mean?"

"Debbie thinks you're great."

True.

"I'm heading home." I checked in with Debbie nightly when I left a place. She worried. But if I called her she at least knew I was still alive.

In the pitch black, I mounted my bike, coasting over trash, broken glass, ripped cardboard lids, discarded milk shakes melted on the pavement. The bar, located in a rotted stretch of city with no streetlights and tin shack dwellings, marked a territory. Lurking in the shadows lived another enemy: the lowlife street urchins with a thriving corner dope business.

A rock hit my front wheel. I slowed, my eyes straining in the dark to see the perpetrator. There were no streetlamps. My headlights lit up foil shacks. "You don't want to do that."

A shine emerged from the dark, circled a Dumpster, hid the pile of small rocks at his feet. He was maybe twelve, no different than the kids I grew up with who threw stones at passing cars, hoping to make dents.

We *could* coexist as neighbors . . . as long as we had an understanding. The Outlaws had no interest in infringing on the shines' street drug trade. But throwing rocks at Outlaws, at a Boss no less . . .

I placed the kid in Basket #2.

I always prepared for The Raid by federal agents. I stashed a phony ID, hid "emergency flight money" in a hole in my floor, lived simply, drove a used Cadillac, and resisted purchasing the $40,000 gazebo. I melted pounds of gold into medallions I gifted as Christmas presents and lived in a brick house (in case of bombs). I devised a remote control starter device for my car and each morning left the front door open just in case of an explosion so I could possibly survive a bomb blast.

The detonation came in the form of Frank's arrest. He, along with thirteen other Outlaws, caught charges for racketeering and drug trafficking. Though I had nothing to do with Frank's extracurricular activities, the whole idea of The Raid and rats gave me mild PTSD and flashed me back to my college days when the Feds had paid me a friendly visit.

"All you did with Frank was move water," Debbie reassured me.

Yes, water. Still, I played it safe. I disappeared temporarily. Life chained to a cell meant intellectual stagnation, extreme loneliness, grainy television soap operas, daily thirty-minute jaunts around caged concrete, and meals shoved through metal slits in the wall.

"It's a burner phone," I told Debbie. "I'm going into seclusion. Turn it on every night between nine and ten. If I need to get ahold of you I'll call you then. Otherwise, keep it off."

"I'm going underground." I left Dozer in charge of club business until it was safe for me to resurface. My options for disguise were limited; still, I shaved my goatee and wore a baseball cap and Ray-Bans. I had no tattoos yet, out of respect for my mom, who hated ink but knew that when she passed I would get them—but only up to the elbow, as long as I worked on the street as an "earner." That way the tattoos could still be covered up if the job required or I needed to evade law enforcement. The last thing I needed was to be easily identifiable.

"Dope is obsolete," I told Jaws when I emerged from hiding two weeks later.

• • •

But it *could* be used as leverage.

The treaty the Hells Angels signed following the flurry of bombings between Outlaws and Hells Angels in the early '90s prohibited the Angels from building a clubhouse in Chicago. They constructed one in Harvey, a southern suburb in Cook County near the Indiana border and Cedar Lake, home to the Invaders, a Hells Angels ally.

Rumors spread that Hells Angels had begun to frequent a Polack bar in Chicago that catered to the Hawks,* a club the Angels' courted. The Outlaws feared that the Angels planned to partner with these support clubs and eventually form a cartel. The painful truth was that we would never be able to *stop* the Hells Angels' reach; but with some small effort (and some ingenuity), we could at least achieve a stalemate.

My goal was "subtle deterrence" with possible "drastic measures." If I was lucky, the results might even be comparable to the infamous "thumb-clipping lesson" that left a Hells Angel's ex-wife's boyfriend mutilated, the thumb displayed for all to remember in a Mason jar.

I targeted several local street gangs, inviting two members at a time to my chiropractor's back office for impromptu meetings.

"Angels are in the city," I opened each conversation. "They're heavy into the dope trade. Their presence might

---

* Later the Hells Angels partnered with the Hawks and formed a cartel.

infringe on your business." Perceived danger induced fear in animals; I hoped the street urchins might make the Angels "disappear."

No Face 13 and 21 Mott Street, were concerned. Two of their leaders came back again and again to "discuss the Angel problem." I used my chiropractor's office for personal safety in case they resorted to unsolicited bloodshed. The doctor didn't care; he was vacationing in the Caribbean.

"I'm not here as an Outlaw," I reminded them. "Our businesses don't conflict. I want us to be friends."

They looked like teenagers; No Face 13's leader shoveled handfuls of M&M's from the candy bowl into his mouth. He grunted his understanding.

The leader of 21 Mott Street paced, stopped in front of the built-in aquarium, pressed his lips to the glass, and mimicked the puffer fish. I focused on the sawed-off shotgun tucked inside Mott Street's trench coat.

Street gangs were a different breed; disorganized, trigger-happy, mostly about twelve, and fierce defenders of their turf. Strategically, it made sense to befriend them. I didn't want them dealing dope with the Angels.

11

THE ANGELS ARE COMING

We weren't Outlaws, we were grown men playing army.

—BIG PETE

A war, even a *fake* one, gave soldiers purpose and a reason to mentally train. It was important the Outlaws believed they were being hunted and so, like a Sunday preacher, I delivered the sermon.

"I've spotted Angels."

The details were disclosed in private one-on-one lunch meetings, with each of the six Bosses from Joliet, Chicago South Side, Kankakee, Elgin, and DeKalb. And even though I never saw a single Angel on my North Side turf, it was important to prepare a decent offense.

"They are hidden in plain sight." I'd gathered the Bosses into my plush North Side office and cranked up The Weather Channel on the TV so the Feds would never pick up my voice.

The Game Plan: Arrange to meet one Boss a week at a predetermined diner or truck stop.

"It's important that we blend." I handed each Boss his respective strip of paper.

"I've written the location on these. When I call you to confirm, just know that we're *actually* meeting three hours later."

"So if you call and say eleven"—Ray Rayner,* Boss of the Elgin chapter, needed further clarification—"we're actually meeting at two?" He stared at me with flat, dull eyes, a look I associated with Rottweilers.

"Right," I shouted as if his hearing were the problem.

"Why don't you just tell us to meet you at two?" Ray Rayner's mouth was still open.

Heat flushed my face. I focused on a strip of tinfoil lining my dropped ceiling. The hum of the air conditioner filled the silence. An equation formed in my head—*Stupid plus stubborn equals Ray Rayner*—and I resisted the urge to slap him.

"I don't like hearing my voice on tape."

I ripped up several dollar bills and gave the various halves to each of the Bosses. "If I ever call to talk to you and there's a problem, give your piece of the dollar to your representative. That person needs to give me your half; if the halves match, I'll talk to them. Otherwise, I won't."

The next week, I stabbed chunks of sausage in the Omega, a greasy diner tucked into a back alley in Addison, and

---

* Ray Rayner was a cast member of *Bozo's Circus,* a show on Chicago's WGN-TV.

Pete in his Chair at Northside clubhouse where he made many decisions; in the background a picture of the history of the club.

glanced at my watch: 2:30. Ray Rayner was late. I knew that somewhere in the clubhouse my cell phone was ringing.

"I tried calling you," Ray Rayner complained later.

"Ever heard of GPS?" I reviewed the play with him again, and the next day sampled moussaka in the Artropolis. Again, he was a no-show.

"What *is* it about this that's so difficult?" I slammed my hand onto the large wooden table, bouncing a mug onto the floor; it shattered into chunks of glass. The five Bosses (minus Santa, who preferred to appear by phone) gathered around my desk, looking like children about to confess.

"You're speaking in code." Big Butch spread out in one of my high-backed leather chairs.

I'm not a sociopath, not really, but my whole body tingles when I want to hurt someone.

Like any great quarterback, I switched tactics.

"There have been Angel sightings, in some of the Polish bars," I lied, though Angels *had* infiltrated the Polish community. "We're going to hunt in packs. Plan to be out all night. The first person who whines is going to wear a probate vest."

I would have preferred a cash fine, but returning someone to slave status packed more punch. I stashed several probate vests on my bike, slipped on a pair of goggles, and geared up for the night watch.

Chapters rolled into the North Side clubhouse dressed for war: black and white vests, checkered bandannas, skull face masks, beards tucked into belts, ponytails secured. We were armed with clubs, chains, knives, and Maglites. Santa and his elves were conspicuously missing. When the rest of the chapters all assembled, we peeled out, a storm of Harleys thundering in the night sky.

First we hit Orion, a Polish restaurant and bar in Garfield Ridge. We parked our bikes in rows curbside, hoping a square might knock one down so we could start a blood trail on the pavement; but really we didn't need a reason. Inside, a DJ spun polka discs beneath decorative red bulbs. The crowded bar, already sticky with spilled beer, filled with smoke. The bartenders were Polish broads, a fact that made it nearly impossible for us to gather intelligence since typically we would have planted our own people inside as surveillance for the club. The waitresses dressed in high spiked boots, heavy lipstick, white blousy tops, scurried around with trays of shot glasses, lowering their gaze as they passed us. One tripped over an Outlaws' boot. A soft mewl escaped her lips as a brother caught her elbow.

"Careful, darling," he said, laughing. "I'll take one of those."

She had a chiseled face and purple highlights in her hair. "No English."

"Crown Royal." I pointed to the bottles along the wall behind the bar.

The tone of my voice attracted attention. Several men turned, drinks in hand, their faces shiny with sweat, their eyes overbright.

"What are you staring at?"

Before I could even react, my enforcer, Iron Mike, shot out like a cartoon boxing glove on a spring. He coldcocked one of the men on the side of his head and dropped him to the floor. Air left the guy's lungs. He lay on his back, eyes startled open, short-cropped blond hair perfectly stiff. Screams erupted. The music skipped. Polish phrases slurred around me.

A drunken free-for-all quickly followed as bodies slammed into walls, heads knocked against tile, and fists pounded flesh. Back doors swung open; patrons rushed into the alley, and the bar transformed from shades of bruised plum to black and white as Outlaws swung wildly with fists and Maglites and stomped random citizens with their steel-toed boots.

I didn't worry about cops. *Chicago was the only place where criminals wore badges.*

•   •   •

We hit a different Polish bar every week. The chapters ro-
tated as we formed a kind of "fight club," perfecting hay-
makers, back fists, hooks, and sucker punches. Sizing up
opponents, jabbing at air, making up insults so we could
retaliate. The rush was better than drugs.

"Can we skip next week?"

I ran cold water over my bloody knuckles. Ray Rayner
peed.

"Maybe it's time to take a break, you know?" He zipped
up his pants.

I dried my fingers on a paper towel, feeling my blood
pressure rise. "We're one-percenters. We don't take breaks."

But I *did* disappear at times, hid in a private villa in a
Chicago suburb, completely blocked from the outside world.
The resort had no windows, no cracks of light, and no
identifying markers on the street. Inside, there were private
waterfalls, steam baths, vibrating Chinese bamboo chair-
lifts. No phone service; no computers, no technology.

"Just forget everything," Backlash said when he first gave
me the villa as a wedding gift. "Go there when you can't stand
it anymore. Stretch it out." He grinned. "If you do everything
at once you'll just be exhausted. Go there and just be Peter."

Just be Pete.

But within minutes of leaving the villa, I morphed again
into character, into Big Pete. At Capri's, Chef Corleone's upscale Italian restaurant, I looked the part, dressed in a
sleeveless black tank, heavy gold rings, black jeans, and

combat boots. I sipped Crown Royal and scanned the crowd of suits and sparkly ladies.

"Pretty fancy place," The Hound remarked. He was one of the few who rode with me that night from Elgin. *It was, and that was the point—to be as disrespectful as possible, to send a message to these wiseguys that we had no fear.*

"I like your tattoos," a broad winked at me, fluttered over, and pulled up a chair. She wore a leather miniskirt and crinkly knee-high boots. "Do you like mine?" She flashed the compass tattoo on her inner thigh. She wore no panties.

"Nice." The Hound licked his lips.

She laughed, tossed back her head, and walked away.

"Let her go," I said. "She'll return."

"I'm going to walk around."

The Hound pushed back from the table; an imposing figure, he waddled to the bar and hovered dangerously close to the broad with the boots. I swallowed my shot. *This wasn't going to end well.*

A patron knocked The Hound's drink to the floor. Whiskey spilled onto his shirt. Punches followed: a hard crack to the patron's lower jaw, a thud to The Hound's ribs. He groaned, doubled over, stumbled a little, and caught the edge of a bar stool.

Concerned for The Hound, I hurled my chair at the patron, spindly metal legs slicing like little knives through flesh. The crowd came alive. Bodies lumped together in a dark mass. Disembodied arms swung and punched like windup toys. After a while my fists burned. Then I heard a crack as my gold-studded fingers smacked against bone. The man's head whipped back and struck the edge of a concrete column, and he crumpled to the floor.

I actually worried I might have killed him, but the fighting continued. Patrons stepped over his neck, circled his body outline. No one checked his pulse. No one moved him out of the way. Blood spotted his scalp. I had my own crisis: One of my gold rings had slipped off.

"Stop!" I boomed. "Don't anyone fucking move."

Patrons froze on the floor in wrestlers' nelson holds. Sweat slicked their faces. All around me, labored breathing, broken glass, a woman's screams. Irish-Italian slang hung in the air. Some in the crowd fled toward the exit.

"Motherfucker, no one leaves."

Sirens exploded in the night. I fixated on people's shoes.

The Hound looked at me. A bruise spread on his cheek like an eggplant.

"I lost my fucking ring."

"Cops are coming," he said.

A waitress crawled on her hands and knees, tears streaming down her face.

"I found it."

I ducked with The Hound into a storage room behind the bar just as the cops stormed in. I pressed an ear to the door.

"My mom will be pissed." The Hound lived with his mother.

"Shhh." I put a finger to my lips. "Be quiet."

"I can't *afford* to go to jail tonight." The Hound popped a can of beer and guzzled it down.

The whole idea behind the bar fights was to create a

presence in the city, maintain an outlaw *image*. I realized in time, as attendance dropped off and fewer and fewer chapters participated in the wildings, that the Outlaws didn't really want to protect the city from Angels. Very few even had the *skills* to be criminals.

Damn, I still had a baggie of coke in my front pocket.

"This is a pretty nice neighborhood," The Hound said. "We're going to look like fucking freaks."

I decided to consume the drugs.

The cops handcuffed us together behind our backs and led us to an SUV.

"I can't climb into that," I said, my heart racing. "I'm too big." *Never mind that The Hound had just managed it.*

Five squad cars parked along the street. Red and blue wigwags lit up The Hound's face. His eyes were watery and bloodshot. The cops huddled, glanced my way and shook their heads.

"If I uncuff you and you bolt, I swear I'll Tase you."

I looked at him, absorbed his fresh clean-cut face, his pudgy blue pants and utility belt, his little cap with the gold piping, and said, "You're fucking kidding, right?"

"Do I look like I have a sense of humor?" The cop uncuffed me.

"Is anyone pressing charges?" I removed my rings one at a time and placed them in the property tray. I already knew no one would. No one would dare. The Outlaws were still considered "one of the most ruthless gangs in the world . . . involved in biking, brotherhood, and bombs."

"You're lucky we don't charge you with use of a weapon." The cop rattled my rings. "These are like brass knuckles."

"Someone probably went to the hospital," The Hound said as we sat on a bench in the booking area, then added, "I have to take a piss."

"Seriously?"

He stood and, because we were attached, I stood too. "You coming?"

"I'm not pissing with you."

A cop uncuffed The Hound, escorted him to the toilet, waited while he pissed, then re-cuffed him with me to the bench. A few minutes later, The Hound raised his hand. "I need to go again." The charade of cuffing and uncuffing The Hound so he could piss continued for another hour, until finally I snapped, "Stop."

"Stop what?"

"Stop pissing."

The Hound dropped his hand, slouched on the bench, swung his feet, and said, "They're not going to press charges, are they?"

"Nope."

"You think this will hit the paper?"

"Probably."

"You think maybe we could skip next week?"

12

RUN

Skipping weeks was **never** an option for an Outlaw, but I could at least switch gears. In between organizing "Angel Hunts" with my fellow Outlaws, I focused on my other responsibilities. As chairman of the COC, I organized "run sheets" (party planning) for thirty-six clubs in the confederation. My goal was to maximize support for each event, streamline costs, and ensure high attendance. With no conflicts, clubs had no excuses; the more participants who showed up at another club's event, the more cash flow, the more visibility for that club, and, ultimately, the more allegiance to me.

Though each club had its individual members governed by a club Boss, *all* followed civil rules of procedure implemented by the board (aka me). Like a federal government trumping state laws, I regulated and organized dysfunction. Bosses from thirty-six clubs in the Chicago area spread their calendars on the conference table. Shines, Polacks, Latinos, Irish, Outlaws all touched shoulders. They were Knight

Keepers, Wanted Mayhem, Tru Dat, Orange Crush, Axemen, Fugarwe Tribe, Gor Gor, Legacy, and on and on.

I went around the table. "Everybody have their fucking dates?"

As each Boss recited time and month, the COC secretary, Yo Adrienne, jotted down notes. Later, she converted the dates to a computerized spreadsheet and distributed the calendar to all clubs. The process involved several days of data entry and cross-checking to avoid duplications.

Yo Adrienne was my perfect foil. Petite and tough, she was a member of the Low Lyfz MC and rode her own Harley. I appointed her because the COC was about nondiscrimination, broads included. And, she was a single mom and needed a job and I liked her.

"Why is a broad calling the shots?" Ray Rayner had promptly tattled to Santa, who'd called me.

"She's my conduit. Anything she says, texts, or otherwise communicates is coming from me exactly as if I were speaking," I told Santa.

"I don't get it."

"Listen, fuckhead, if you think for one minute I would allow a broad to order brothers around . . ."

"But she is."

"I'm telling her what to say."

"Oh . . . like a ventriloquist?"

I hung up.

"Runs" were not just parties, they were moneymaking opportunities and meet and greets. Any scheduling questions or issues I deferred to the secretary; any serious fuckups, it was "Yo, Adrienne, fix it."

But it was hard to fix stupid. Ray Rayner sent his flunky, Scooter, to the meetings for scheduling purposes and, in case it somehow wasn't obvious, assured us, "Anything Scooter does, says, or communicates is at Ray Rayner's command."

Exactly as if Ray Rayner were speaking.

As a rule I paid little attention to Ray Rayner or his Elgin chapter; both were a source of irritation. But since he occasionally contributed to moneymaking enterprises . . . he wasn't completely useless.

Scooter focused on a dark spot in the ceiling. It was the same stare I had seen on the televangelist Jim Bakker when he paused for dramatic effect disguised as boredom, or simply lost his place, or forgot a crucial part of his speech. Scooter, the wannabe Ray Rayner, Bozo the Clown lookalike, with his shock of bright orange hair, Fu Manchu mustache, and giant, almost grotesque, hands, had "forgot" his calendar.

"We usually have two runs, one in May, the other in September. . . ." His voice trailed off; he left the room to make a phone call.

"You're holding up the meeting." I snarled. The Outlaws looked ridiculous. I wanted to appear fair, but in fact I favored the Outlaws. Everyone else had come prepared. They'd brought their calendars. They'd planned their runs.

Scooter returned minutes later. "I can't get ahold of anyone."

"Do you want me to wait for his dates?" Yo Adrienne asked.

"No, put his party as a footnote."

Ray Rayner called the next day. "I have the dates—the runs will happen on the twentieth." He sounded sure.

"You embarrassed the Outlaws in front of all the other clubs," I began my tirade, rambling on and on until finally he cut me off: "It won't happen again."

"No, it won't."

He called a week later. "I made a mistake. Our runs are actually on the eighteenth."

"Will that be another footnote?" Yo Adrienne revised the run sheet again, adding footnotes and asterisks.

"I think you're missing the point of the run sheets," I said, pulling Bozo the Clown aside. "We *want* the support clubs to come to our parties and spend their money. They *support* the Outlaws. But if we don't tell them *when* our runs happen, they can't come. And we'll lose revenue. Understand?"

Ray Rayner hosted Elgin's party that weekend.

He introduced his bodyguard. "He's on me tonight." Bozo's muscle was the size of a fat building; he had no neck, arms like tree stumps, and looked like he had been recruited from a movie set to play "The Thug."

"What do you mean?" I said.

"He'll make sure nobody gets to me."

"Who's going to *get* to you?" First of all, it was *Elgin,* thirty-five miles northwest of Chicago. Its tallest building was a Kmart. "You're in an Outlaw clubhouse. Do you honestly think someone is going to assassinate you here?" *Besides, you're not important. Nobody shoots the fourth-in-charge.*

13

LIFE OF THE PARTY

Finally, it was my turn. A party was a production, a carefully staged play that began with perception and costume. And so, in the quiet of my bedroom, curtains drawn, I morphed into character, became my own darker version of me. I put on my costume, pulled on my black T-shirt and jeans, laced up my combat boots, and headed downstairs to sit in my high-backed leather office chair. I loosened my belt just enough to slip in my KA-BAR straight-edged knife.

Next, I rubber-banded my thick ponytail every two inches so my hair would not tangle and adjusted my bandanna above my jeweled earrings, two one-carat diamond studs in the left ear, a white gold hoop with five diamonds in the right.

"How does this look?"

Debbie smiled. "Good."

I clasped my heavy gold "Charlie" medallion around my neck; black and white diamonds encircled the skull, with two ruby eyes. I slipped on my vest, tucked two pistols into hidden slits sewn inside the fabric, shoved cigarettes and a lighter in the right pocket and slid my phone into the left. Last, I put on my rings; several pounds of gold bands adorned my fingers. My index fingers I kept free in case I had to pull a trigger.

I mounted my bike, gunned the engine, and rode full throttle up my street, flipped a U-turn and waved to Debbie. I repeated this maneuver at least three times, sometimes making a sharp left turn, then a right, weaving in and out of nearby neighborhoods, hoping to ward off snipers and potential stalkers.

Meanwhile, Debbie stood in the doorway, arms crossed, brow wrinkled.

"Be safe," she said. "Call me when you're headed home."

Crowds formed at the entrance to the North Side clubhouse. Enforcers taped yellow adhesive to the floor, circling my chair as if I were a crime scene.

I sat center stage, surrounded by Kreepy Tom, Sick Bastardo, Mr. Happy. Partygoers lined up like therapy patients, shook my extended hand, gushed about the opportunity to consult with "Big Pete," thanked me for listening to their problems, and waited their turn to speak, trancelike, eyes rolled back, as if my very touch

Pete's throne

transformed them. Some stood for a minute and a half before me, others more than eight, depending on how important they were.

Some flashed their tits, thrust black Sharpies in my hand, and asked me for an autograph.

"Nice to see you," I'd say, but I *didn't* see them; instead I studied the room the way a general notes exits, blended faces, and subtle shifts in expression.

"Back the fuck up," Bastardo would say, shoving the faces pressed too close to my space.

More people grabbed my outstretched hand. "Thanks for the birthday wishes," I repeated over and over, though it wasn't my birthday. No one noticed. *Wrong script, wrong play, wrong presentation.* The room shrunk small as a television. "Heard you like red velvet candy." A broad with thick black braids grinned and offered up the bag of melts wedged between her breasts. Another straddled my lap and whispered in the shell of my ear, "I wore loose jeans just for you."

"Okay, sweetheart, take two steps back." My breath came in short, fast bursts, my claustrophobia crippling me.

"Thanks for the Christmas gift." More strangers shook my hand, *though it wasn't Christmas.*

I glanced at Bastardo, and he must have registered my pained expression.

"Not too many more, Boss."

The line snaked into the back room. Women stared at me, their gaze so intense I began to feel like the last donut on the shelf. I listened to domestic issues, financial problems, health crises, as hours ticked by and my voice cracked.

"I can't sleep, man," one brother said, sucking cigarette after cigarette, his eyes all scratched up with thin red lines. "I keep thinking they're coming for me, you know? Every car that backfires—*bang!*" his voice exploded. "You know what I mean?"

I did. I really did. I wanted to tell him to lay off the coke, but instead I advised him, "Get a dog."

A probate approached, his right eye swollen and waxy yellow. Though he stood in the middle of the room, inside the circle of yellow tape, he spoke freely, as if we were alone.

"I got three kids." His voice faltered. "One of them died last year."

He looked like he hadn't seen sunlight in months. His skin had a grayish tint, suggesting slow decay.

"You need to go home." I knew what it was like to lose a child: My own daughter no longer spoke to me. "This life," I began. "It takes casualties."

He stared at me, his mouth open.

"You can't be here," I said. "Your child *died*. Your mind is elsewhere."

The probate looked confused.

"Outlaws don't have *feelings*."

He started to protest but I cut him off. "Being an Outlaw is a lifestyle, it's a choice. Most of us are here because we don't fit into the square world. We don't *want* to fit in, see?"

The probate nodded.

"The club is our family. The brothers come first. God, country, your dog, even your old lady are secondary. You don't get weekends off. There are no time-outs, you understand?"

"But," the probate protested.

"You're a liability. You have three kids still at home. You'll be thinking about *them* instead of protecting your brothers."

A welt beneath his eye split and fresh blood oozed out.

Behind him, near the bar, a drunken citizen bumped the shoulder of an Outlaw, spilled the contents of his paper cup onto the Outlaw's steel-toed boot. Mr. Happy already had the guy in a headlock and, on my cue, punched him hard in both eyes before tossing him into the alley.

"I get it," the probate nodded. "I'll think about it."

He had six months: 179 days, 23 hours, and 59 minutes.

As the night wore on and the crowd thinned, Bastardo disclosed he had just pierced his penis, a detail I found perplexing, since he had no other holes in his skin. But that wasn't his issue.

"Do you think it's normal for a broad to want her ribs bruised during foreplay?" I had to think about that; I knew of many who enjoyed rough sex, even asphyxiation. Hell, I had once lifted a broad by her throat and squeezed so hard the capillaries in her eyes burst. And when she hit the floor hard, nearly passed out, she'd sputtered, "Is that all you got?"

"I think the girl might have issues," I said to Bastardo.

Maybe we all did? Behind him a few midgets strapped Velcro harnesses to their chests and encouraged drunken Outlaws to hurl them against concrete to see if they might stick.

I lost track of time. Kreepy Tom brought me water in a paper cup. My legs numbed from sitting too long.

Chuck, in between summaries of *Green Acres* reruns, announced his preference for BDSM* and asked if I wanted to meet Lady Sarah (his BDSM dominatrix). *Maybe.*

Chuck, who resembled a coke machine with a head, also wanted a tattoo, "a teardrop on my face."

"You can't have one."

"Why not?"

"Because you haven't killed anyone." *And you haven't been to prison, and you're not mourning the loss of a loved one, and . . .*

"I want one."

"What the fuck, Chuck," I said.

"I like the way they look."

"It means something." Never mind that *any* face tattoos would make him immediately memorable to the police.

Chuck looked like he was about to explode. I knew he ingested steroids like candy but tonight he looked wired, hyped, and his nose leaked. He once boasted about taking ninth place in a weight-lifting competition, and I couldn't help but wonder what color the ninth-place ribbon looked like.

---

* Bondage and discipline, sadism and masochism

Lady Sarah nudged him. She was a stocky bodybuilder type and spoke with a lisp. She smiled at me, handed me a Sharpie, and asked if I would autograph her left tit. Chuck lived with his old lady in her basement. Twenty years his senior, she towered over him at a freakish six-seven.

"Lady Sarah sits on my face sometimes." He grinned. "I like it."

"Only with my jeans on," Lady Sarah said as she slapped him playfully on the shoulder.

My hand shook as I scribbled "You're welcome, Big Pete" on her tit.

"Hope I see you around." She winked at me.

"Do you ever think of *me* like that?" The next broad in line cocked her head to the side and fluttered her lashes. The lids blinked "Fuck me."

"Sure." I smiled. "I'm thinking I'd like to smash a brick into your face and turn it into a hamburger." She looked a little startled, laughed uneasily.

"There's no way you and I are getting together, see? I don't care if you can suck a golf ball through a straw." She sashayed away as if retreating from some invisible line that marked the end of one life and the beginning of another—one I never crossed. Sex was not my aphrodisiac.

"Don't let the small legs fool you. What you see is not what you get." A midget twirled in front of me.

"Darling, you have nothing I desire." I wasn't being cruel, just blunt. She sucked in her cheeks, reminding me of the broad I once slammed through a window after I found her fashioning a crack pipe out of a showerhead.

"I'm sure you've never had a lap dance the way I could give you one." She trailed her fingers along my vest. Something alive in me snapped. My reaction pure reflex, I slammed her head into my knee. Her nose cracked. She looked up at me as a dark bruise formed underneath her eye.

"I don't like to be touched."

Bastardo nudged me. "Look who just walked in: the night's release." We called them "The Tens"—one was tall and lean, the other fat and round like the number zero. They winked at the row of brothers propped against the wall, grabbed some drinks, and strayed into a back room. The men lined up, one by one, for blow jobs, like they were waiting to use the same urinal. They turned the activity into sport and a competition of who could go the longest without exploding. Claps and cheers and gulps followed, along with a mock countdown: "Ten, nine, eight," the men chanted with no pants on until the semen glistened on the Tens' bellies and thighs. Some returned for seconds and thirds, and when the Tens emerged, smelly, sweaty, barely human anymore, Cockroach gave each a long, sloppy tongue kiss.

"I'm heading home." I said.

At the top of the Sears Tower, Chicago lit up the night like my personal Christmas tree. She spread wide, waiting for me to enter her like a lover bursting with secrets. Here, I could be completely alone, utterly myself. The air was so thin, I had to learn to breathe again.

Soon it would be Debbie's birthday. I decided to buy her a star.

14

THE OTHER ME

My home *fit* me. Oversized sofas circled a television on the wall the size of a movie screen, dwarfing my large frame. My tub resembled a Jacuzzi. Here, like valves releasing steam, I decompressed. The layers of Big Pete, Outlaw Boss, peeled off, leaving just Pete.

"Full moon is coming in two days." Debbie actually marked the date on the calendar. She warned our neighbors and friends. That was their cue to disappear.

"If he goes off, don't make eye contact," Debbie told them.

I paced the halls, rage building inside me, thoughts blowing through the dark, wide spaces; ghostly faces pressed against glass behind my heavy bedroom curtains.

I ripped electric cords from the walls. *Help me,* the voices whispered. I smashed bulbs suspended from the ceiling, knifed my couch until foam spewed from the cushions.

"You okay in there?" Debbie would call.

• • •

A week later Lady Sarah sent me a photo: Whip in hand, she straddled a client bound at the wrists and ankles with leather straps, a death head-tattoo stretching across his chest.

"We should meet," I said when I called her later, not at all interested in her *skills,* but in her clientele. If she could lure Hells Angels and other prominent rivals into her dungeon, the earning and intelligence-gathering potential would be huge.

Business was business, after all.

Lady Sarah wore a tight corset that revealed her considerable chest, thigh-high spiky boots decorated down the sides with grommets, and a miniskirt.

"Want a tour?"

I stepped inside "The Dungeon," a cavelike dwelling easily accessible from the airport and the Loop. The place, immaculate and inviting, divided into several play spaces, each with a theme and purpose, well-equipped and secluded. A sign above the door read, "I am your sin. I am your soul. I am."

Clients ordered off the menu, fantasies I could never imagine: coprophilia, ruby showers (menstrual urine), mummification, toilet slaves, and special restraints that included plastic wraps, body bags, even a latex vacuum bed. Other offerings, like "ball busting," cage and rope bondage, straitjackets, and "sploshing," were available upon request.

Lady Sarah cut right to the chase. "I'm looking for a partner. A financier. I work five days a week and pull in two to four sessions a day. If you help me, you could earn a thousand dollars a week or more."

I was in.

Being an Outlaw was expensive—weekly club dues, tombstone taxes every time a brother passed (and sometimes there were multiple deaths in one month), national dues, contributions to the legal defense fund, event fees (which only increased for brothers if they invited their old ladies).

The role of Lady Sarah's muscle required little effort. She serviced influential people—Bosses, CEOs, high-ranking mobsters, lawyers, government officials: "wonderfully brilliant men" who sometimes needed reminders that she was in charge. Being a dominatrix was risky business; Lady Sarah had information on people that made her a killing target.

"It's exhausting always being the leader," Lady Sarah explained domme-submissive psychology to me. "These men come to me to escape from life's stresses. The theatrical fantasies of sexual surrender offer a release, a vacation, from always being in charge." Her beautiful brown eyes sparkled. "It's a hell of a lot cheaper than going to the Bahamas, I promise you."

But not all of her clients suffered from an imbalance in power. Some were just kinky regular folk—blue-collar workers, cabdrivers, *bikers* who needed to feel desired for a few hours.

"She's stealing my clients," Lady Sarah complained one day about her rival, Midnight High, a veteran domme whose dungeon was just a few blocks away.

I made an agreement with the rival, borrowing my favorite line from *The Godfather*: "Either you put your name on a noncompete contract, or I'll put your brains on it."

I never had to say much; mine were subtle threats. Midnight High moved on.

I recruited alone, scoured the fashion shows for prospects. My goal was to lure five or six girls at a time into the escort business and offer each some reprieve from the murky world of pole dancing. Rapport was an art; I knew the girls had handlers.

Broads paraded around me in tight-cropped tops, fitted jeans, spiked heels, their doll-like eyes with fake-glued lashes blinking in the harsh lights. Some looked chiseled, like carved stone.

Most strippers had been numbed to the bait—squatty bald men in white muscle shirts who tossed small bills and coins onto their stage. I looked for the moths, the fragile, soft creatures that clung to the walls, waited near the exits, and slowly, slowly flew toward the flame.

I began in the rural areas, where dancers earned less than $2 a move. I studied them as if they were rare finds that required modest refurbishing. Dressed in full Outlaw regalia, I wanted to appear like dipped gold.

A few fluttered around me. One was a pixie waif with dry blond hair, drugged-out eyes. I shooed her away: "When I want you to come over, I'll ask."

Soon, another came, and another, until I'd collected six or seven rescues, the score reminding me of the time when, in the seventh grade, while my classmates glued pretty butterflies onto presentation boards, I cut up a cockroach into six different parts and stuck the bits and pieces onto cardboard:

wings, legs, an eye, a head. I told the teacher, "The wind blew apart their insides." The teacher smiled at me, patted me on the head, and praised my "resourcefulness," my ability to make something out of nothing.

Some mornings, instead of recruiting, I rode my bike through deserted alleys, crushed littered cans with my tires and marveled at the unique plate-glass towers, rows and rows of red-brick buildings and ghostly steel spires that jutted into the skyline, claiming "The White City" as its own among the clouds. Marked by resilience and strength, the progressive structures rose from the ashes of the Great Chicago Fire, determined to "not be derivative, not follow the status quo."* Buildings on the outskirts, *Beware!*

Riding alone was Zen-like; the city absorbed into my skin. I became fully aware of just being in the moment. And with my senses heightened, I could taste the sky, see the color of the wind, feel the vibration of the bike as if it were my very life beat. The Outlaws MC insignia looked like it was sewn onto the tank. My beloved Chicago skyline, including the Sears Tower, covered one chrome fender, and on the front shined the one-percenter diamond.

Chinatown, with its neon signs, ornate pagodas, and gold-painted buildings, offered a kind of tenderloin. Dragon kites blew from bank windows. Red paper lanterns rattled in the wind. The whole town felt thin, like something make-believe, a child's garish painting.

---

* "Chicago's Architectural History," by Dennis McKnight

Pete's Bike

I rode to a massage parlor. A flurry of dainty, porcelain-like broads stripped my boots, soaked my feet, placed wet cucumbers over my eyelids as I tumbled into a dark hole, a hole I alone inhabited. Here, the stress of acting human fell away. When I emerged an hour later, transformed, jellylike, I rode to the campus of College of DuPage, where I audited philosophy classes on negotiating and logic. One required text was *Alice in Wonderland*. I devoured the book, high-lighted passages, memorized whole sections, admired the White Rabbit, and when the final exam came and contained only one question, "Why?" I wrote, "Why Not?"

By the time I arrived at "work" in the late afternoon, my chapter was just starting to wake. No brothers guessed my other life; as far as they knew, I slept in, exhausted from the night before.

• • •

But I was never refreshed enough to deal with Das Jew, a fixture in the Outlaw biker community, an old-timer who quit the club once the bombings started in 1995 and later rejoined when he deemed it "safe" to be an Outlaw again. He reminded me of the cop who craved the title but feared the role and hid instead in his local elementary school as a D.A.R.E. officer, hoping no one noticed.

Das Jew worked at McCormick Place, a massive convention center near the shore of Lake Michigan and just a few kilometers south of downtown Chicago. He was useful, employed a lot of bikers and mob guys in various jobs with the teamsters, riggers, and Decorators Union, doing ghost payrolls, forklift work, and other jobs.

"He's here *again*?" I said.

Bastardo grinned. "Fucking mama's boy."

"I need to talk to you." Das Jew's large-framed glasses slipped down the bridge of his nose. He followed me into my office, his boots clicking on the hickory floor. He blinked at me, his eyes wet and overbright. It was truly beyond me that his ol' lady was a bank vice president. I had no clue why Das Jew was in my office, except maybe to kiss my ass.

"What's up?" It was like my whole body was braced for his impact.

"It's my mom." His voice caught, and then it was all over. He dissolved into sobs, convulsive, inconsolable crying.

I shut my office door. It was far too early in the afternoon for me to practice compassion, but Das Jew was never going to leave if I didn't at least pretend to care.

"Sit down," I said, motioning to a chair. "When did she pass?"

Pete pouring Crown Royal with gold rings, index finger bare so he can pull a trigger.

Das Jew wiped his runny nose with the back of his hand. "Six years ago."

Six years ago? Why was the fucker still crying?

"Sorry, Boss, I just miss her, you know?"

I did know.

But what did it matter?

Hitler loved his mother too.

15

GUNS N' ROSES

"Hey, I know you," the broad with white hair and rope tattoos shouted across the bar. I sat at my same corner table again, hidden in plain sight, sipping a shot of Crown Royal. Soon Mr. Happy, Bastardo, The Hound, and Junior joined me.

The Hound grinned. "Look who's back."

"I thought we went through this already," I said to the broad.

She stumbled toward me holding a rose. Her strange brown eyes had flecks of gold like crushed glass in them. She was bone-thin; her skin barely tucked in her ribs.

"We've met," she said, then coughed.

Did she once work for me? After a while they all blended together.

"I don't like you." She twirled the stem. A thorn pricked her thumb, and a trickle of blood bubbled out.

"There's nothing I like about you either."

Mr. Happy gulped his glass of warm water. If I ordered him, he would drop the waif to the floor and pistol-whip her with the butt of his Glock until it broke apart. But there was something spooky about this broad, like she was a ghost from my Christmas Past and had a message for me.

She handed me the rose.

"What's this for?"

"A peace offering."

The Hound sat back and stretched. Most broads he devoured; this one he just looked at, as if marveling at the various "packages" women came in.

"No thanks."

"It won't hurt you."

The bar grew suddenly quiet. The few people inside stopped to watch the showdown involving the flower. A large, pasty-faced farm boy with a drawl blurted out, "Take the fucking rose, asshole."

Mr. Happy shot to his feet.

I took the rose, motioned for Mr. Happy to stay put. I slid my chair back. Farm Boy didn't move. Instead he took a long pull from his beer. The waif slipped into the shadows.

Behind me, guns racked.

I walked up to Farm Boy, smiled.

"Say it again. I didn't hear you the first time."

Farm Boy swallowed, swiveled to face me, and said, "You're an asshole."

I whipped the rose across his face. Petals exploded around him. Then the punches flew, random, swift, hard, and not just from Farm Boy. Patrons tumbled out of nowhere. I swung wildly, striking anyone that moved. Screams erupted. A pool stick shattered the front window. Mr. Happy

tossed an assailant across the counter like a human bowl-
ing ball headed full force into stacked pins.

I dropped Farm Boy to the floor, surrounded by roses. I
squeezed his throat, fascinated as the tiny capillaries in his
eyes popped brighter.

Mr. Happy pulled me off him and said, "We need to go."

Sirens sawed the night. Ambulances alarmed. The bar
resembled debris from a bomb blast. The bar mirror shattered, and in the shards of broken glass our reflections elon-
gated like a jagged Picasso.

We scrambled into the waiting van and Mr. Happy
gunned the engine.

"Did everyone make it?" Bleary-eyed from booze and
fight, I did a quick head count. "Where's Junior? How am I
the first one in here?" Junior threw himself on top of me and
Mr. Happy sped off. We only made it a block.

A black suburban and five squad cars blocked our path.
Wig-wags lit up our faces. Cops surrounded us, their weapons
drawn. An entire SWAT team dressed in full riot gear, bulletproof vests, metal-plated knee pads, Kevlar skull helmets,
and chin guards piled out of the squad cars and formed a
perimeter around our van.

"They're doing this because we're Outlaws." Junior
sounded drunk.

"Of course they're doing this because we're Outlaws." I
stashed the knives.

One aimed his holographic-sight-equipped M4 carbine rifle
at the windows; he was completely sleeved, with a colored

rose tattoo covering the back of his hand. Skulls and letters dotted every knuckle.

The Chicago Police Department once tried to "professionalize" the uniforms, but many cops balked, claiming "the general public already view[ed] [them] as robots." One Irish beat cop insisted his tattoos "were part of my identity, my heritage. They have no impact on the way I perform my duties as a Chicago police officer."

"The fuckers look like *us*," The Hound said. *I was pretty sure they wanted to* be *like us, too.*

These tattooed members of the police department, the so-called Sons of Anarchy, formed close and "unprofessional" relationships with members of outlaw motorcycle gangs, ironically actually *creating* anarchy in their own departments.

"Open up," a cop boomed through the blow horn.

Mr. Happy stepped out first, hands in the air, unlit cigarette dangling from his lips.

The van doors shot open and one by one cops ordered us to "drop to the ground." The Hound and I didn't really "drop"; we stumbled, and slowly lowered ourselves to a kneeling position.

"What happened?" Officer Deric stared at us through fitted black goggles.

No one said a word. I focused on the potholes and the many subtle grooves in the road that could tip a bike. The Hound breathed heavily beside me; he wasn't having a panic attack, but sometimes just the sheer exertion of changing positions could make a man his size wheeze.

"I'll ask it again; What happened back there?"

My knees, through denim, bit into the gravel. "We got jumped."

The cop flipped up his goggles. "Is that so?"

I shrugged.

"How come six of them are headed to the hospital?"

"We didn't start the fight," I said.

"So this was self-defense?" The cop rolled his eyes.

Mr. Happy's hands still had streaks of blood on them. His knuckles swelled from the force of his punches. I was pretty sure Farm Boy was one of the ones headed to the hospital.

"Lucky for you no one's pressing charges." Officer Deric lowered his voice, leaned in close, and pulled a "Bonasera"* move: "You know that I know that we know what really happened here, right?"

---

* Amerigo Bonasera, from Mario Puzo's *The Godfather*

16

LOBSTER SAUCE

Crime does pay . . . just not forever.

—BIG PETE

One midnight, a few of us sat around the South Side clubhouse playing Monopoly, although most of the players had
already declared bankruptcy, one remained in jail, and I had
mortgaged all of the properties. Orange cones and red plastic hotels dotted the board. And I commandeered the bank
of paper money.

"This game sucks," What the Fuck Chuck whined. "I've
been sitting in jail for five turns."

"Let's order pizza," Mountain said. I could tell he had
had enough. "Little Caesars, five pizzas for five bucks."

"I'm not eating that shit," I said.

Mountain rolled his eyes. "What would you prefer—"

"Lobster," I cut him off. I felt it my duty to establish
a standard. *This was my theater, after all, and I was the
director.*

"Lobster?" Mountain snorted. "Where are you going to get fish this time of night?"

"Lobster is not fish." I snapped my fingers at Mr. Happy. He dialed Tony's place. The year before Tony had been kidnapped and held for ransom. His ol' lady ran his restaurant now.

"Order fifteen," I said.

"Fifteen lobsters this time of night?" Mountain shook his head.

"Just do it." I was proving a point. Never mind that it was the South Side and no one in his right mind traveled into these neighborhoods after dark. The clubhouse stood adjacent to a vacant lot, surrounded by a brick wall with barbed wire along the perimeter.

An hour and twelve buzzer rings later, (to make the delivery boy sweat) several packages of iced lobster arrived in the clubhouse. I slapped $775 cash into the delivery boy's hands.

"You forgot the garlic bread," I said, though I hadn't even looked. The clubhouse went still. No one spoke. The boy's face paled. He shifted uncomfortably from one leg to the other. He opened his mouth to speak, and a few apologies stuttered out.

"Go back and bring it to us." I shut the door. I didn't expect him to return.

"Did the lobsters make it?" Tony's restaurant called to confirm.

I spread containers of butter over the bar counter and dipped a tail in. "Yep." I sucked out the fresh white meat and licked my fingers. "If the boy gets back, tell him not to bother."

I rolled home around three in the morning, having consumed so much lobster I had practically *become* one.

"You smell like butter," Debbie said.

Hours later, the partying began again: A flurry of people waited in line for "advice," some stripped to their underwear, "bug-free," their phone batteries tossed in the Dumpster. *"We love you, Pete"* postcards littered my desk, showing half-naked broads flashing, with spread legs, pouty lips, busty chests, and bottles of Crown Royal shoved deep into parts of them I'd only imagined existed.

"A few prizes out there." Bastardo salivated.

"How would you know?" Fatigue had hit me already. Truth: I hated parties.

"I may have test-run a few."

"Then I'm definitely not interested. And even if I *was* looking," I stressed, "the fact that a broad has slept with other Outlaws makes her even less appealing."

"Come on."

"Soldiers don't send girls *up* the chain." I'd had this "pecking order" conversation with him before—broads who were not already their ol' man's property showed up at clubhouses for one purpose: to participate in orgies.

"Sodom and Gomorrah," I said, pointing out "The Tens," who showed up every Wednesday—"Hump Day"—to service Outlaws in the bathroom.

"I'm not following," one Boss said, shaking his head when I voiced my concerns about the orgies at a Church meeting.

"I'm asking you to tone it down."

"What the fuck for?"

"We don't need heat."

"My goal"—he thumped his chest like a card-toting Neanderthal—"is to sleep with *everyone*. I'm nondiscriminatory. Isn't that what you preach?"

"You're conflating goals."

"Conflating?" He frowned.

"Mixing ideas," I overenunciated.

"I know what the word means. Why do you got to be such an asshole?"

Maybe it was my own need for retribution; after all, it had once been my goal too—to sample every race. But I had been in college. And after two-hundred-plus girls, I'd stopped counting. And I wasn't out to *hurt* them. And I wasn't yet married. And . . . and . . . and . . .

But I was a Boss. My position made my moral stance a little tricky.

It was one thing to watch three Outlaws duck into the toilet in my clubhouse to ingest lines of coke and scold them to get the fuck out. That was about protection in case of a raid; I wasn't about to go down with the flagship. Drugs were not a sanctioned club activity. More like fringe benefits.

A broad appeared in the doorway. She bit her lower lip, a puffy scar lining her cheek, her T-shirt torn. Her friend drifted into the shadows, into the forest of wolves. (Later, she would stumble home, bloodstained, numb, and swollen with secrets.) I learned to compartmentalize, not to let go, but to block.

"You make me feel so special," the broad in the doorway beamed.

"Why is that?"

"I've always wanted to be with an Outlaw, but I never imagined I could be with the *head* Outlaw."

I motioned for her to take a seat.

"Do you know why I love you so much?" she gushed.

"Look, it's never going to happen." Her smile instantly vanished.

Careful, Pete. I owned three escort businesses, but my assistant, Angel, managed them for me. I just made *appearances,* occasionally bought the girls fancy dinners, sported them to shopping sprees, and hired Outlaws to be their drivers. They worked for me because they *liked* me.

"You're the only person who's ever asked me what I wanted," the broad stuttered. It was true. I counseled several of them, permanently "solved" problems with ex-husbands and secured back child support, using "any means necessary." I had a soft spot for moms. Anywhere I went in Chicago, I had exclusive rights over the broads.

"Nothing in the world is going to get us together."

Later, she sent me naked postcards.

"Another stalker?"

"It's not funny." I'd ordered cheese and meatballs at Bastardo's Italian restaurant, Genco.* It was a little early for

---

* Genco is the name of the olive oil store in *The Godfather.*

lunch, Ray Rayner's voice pinging in my head from the night before: *We have a little problem.* . . .

"I like you, Lou," I said to Bastardo, using his real name. My head throbbed.

Bastardo slid across from me, stocky, bald, and sporting his customary dark-tinted glasses. He tugged at a loose thread on his patch that read "CDC" ("Cunts Don't Count").

"But you've *got* to stop fucking Scotty's ex-broad."

Bastardo stroked his goatee. "*This* is what you wanted to see me about?"

"Look, *personally* I don't care about the broad. It's Dino. He's pissed at Scotty's ex. He's gone a little berserk." The waitress placed a steaming plate in front of me. "He's stalking her on social media."

"He's a pussy."

I twirled melted cheese on my fork. "*The broad's* the problem. She's a liability, and could sue."

"I like her." Bastardo folded his arms across his chest.

I swallowed slowly. "Then don't let Dino find out. If he catches you together then your problem becomes *my* problem."

"I get it."

"Don't back me into a corner. . . ."

"I won't."

But two weeks later Ray Rayner spotted Bastardo with the broad again.

"I thought we discussed this," I said, having returned to Genco's.

"We did." Bastardo shrugged. "I decided to keep her. I offered to settle up with Dino man-to-man, but he refused."

In the biker world, there was no such thing as "man-to-man"; it was always "club-to-club."

"A Black Piston just challenged an Outlaw to a fight," Ray Rayner pointed out the obvious.

"You have to go," I said to Bastardo. "I'm exiling you."

"You're kidding, right?"

"I hope she's worth it."

"Shadow me," I instructed Mr. Happy. I planned to groom him for the position of Boss, and figured if others saw him with me all the time they would naturally think of him as my closest advisor, entrusted to make decisions on my behalf. He made the perfect sidekick: poker-faced, clean-cut, perpetually sober.

"He looks like a fucking cop," Frog said as he smoothed the few strands of hair left on his head. He was a junk collector by trade, and took pride in sniffing out "trash."

"He's not a cop."

"An infiltrator then."

"He's my Hand."

"Your *what*?"

"My *Hand*, asshole, my *Hand*."

"Whatever, he's still a Polack."

There were times when I fantasized about turning a person's head into a canoe.

Mr. Happy lapped up my commands—"Stay"; "Sit"; "Guard"; "Attack"—obeying without hesitation.

Once, I ordered Mr. Happy to stay in the van while I attended Church in the Metropolis. "Don't move," I said. "For anyone. As soon as this meeting is over I'm climbing back into this van."

Members from the chapter in Joppa, Illinois, packed into a small room inside their clubhouse. Some lit cigarettes, and a veil of smoke wafted above our heads. People pushed, shoved, and clamored over others just to wedge inside the door.

"Some asshole probate is blocking the entrance to this place." A probate from the Joppa chapter popped his head in.

"Tell him to move," I shrugged.

"He refuses. Says he won't move unless his Boss tells him it's okay."

Oh boy.

"Who's his Boss?" a Joppa member asked.

"Big Pete," I piped up.

"Never heard of him," the enforcer shook his head.

Now I was pissed.

"What the fuck?" I went outside to the van. The enforcer trotted after me. I stopped. "What are you doing?"

"I'm . . . enforcing." He looked ridiculous, a little guy playing a tough guy in a puffy man's costume.

"Enforce this, you big fuck." I punched him in the head, and he fell to the pavement. "Maybe next time you'll remember I'm a motherfucker."

"You told me not to move." Mr. Happy glanced at Mr. Enforcer, out cold.

"Yes I know, but—"

"So, I'm not moving."

Later, I counseled Mr. Happy. "Don't do that again."

"But—"

"Don't be so stubborn."

He sighed. "Maybe this *isn't* for me after all?"

17

BURNING DOWN THE HOUSE

It's not my fucking fault I turned out this way—I'm
a purebreed.

—BIG PETE

The Fugarwe Tribe hosted their annual party at their clubhouse. Inside, a small crowd formed. Members from Brothers
Rising, the Loyal Order, Twisted Image, Low Lyfz, and
stragglers clustered against a far wall. The place, which resembled a storage unit, reeked of sweat and stale beer. A
four-foot caiman crocodile splashed behind the bar, cooling
in his plastic pool.

Voices popped around me like radio static. Smoke made
my eyes burn. I grabbed a shot of Crown Royal and sipped
it slowly, always careful never to lose control while I worked.
I felt closed in, constricted, even a little nervously excited,
like the buzz I got just before a football game.

The jukebox blasted classic rock tunes in a corner. I hovered near the pool table with Mr. Happy, who looked every bit

the porn star, with his perfectly blond coiffed mustache, clean pressed jeans, and unblemished skin. He could have stepped off a movie set. I scanned the room for slight movement, a slip of a hand inside a pocket, a stocking cap wedged beneath an armpit, a stumbling drunk who bumped into the wrong brother. Like watching ripples on a lake, noting which stones skipped, which sunk, which skimmed and caused waves.

My gaze strayed to the floor, to the baggie of fine white powder at my feet. I couldn't help myself; I was still, after all, an opportunist. It wasn't weakness or addiction that drew me to the baggie—it was challenge and intrigue. And, truth be told, if someone was going to be so careless as to drop a baggie, who was I to pass it up? I nudged Jaws, and he hid the baggie with his boot. My heart raced at the thought of the score.

Jaws grinned and pulled out his keys, and, in a dark corner, dipped the groove into the powder and inhaled. He coughed, shook his head. His eyes watered.

"It's not cocaine, Boss," he sputtered. "It's chalk, from the pool table."

Slim, ex-Boss of the Fugarwes, bumped Crazy Tom's elbow, an unforgivable insult that nearly knocked the Outlaw into a wall. But before Crazy Tom could recover his balance, Slim flipped over the Outlaw's gold "Charlie" medallion—a Christmas gift—and patted the skull necklace: "Charlie's backwards."

Slim was done. Club Rule #1: Never touch an Outlaw. Club Rule #2: Never insult the club. Club Rule #3: Refer to Club Rule #1. Club Rule #4: Retribution must follow.

Pete with Medallion

I swallowed the shot, wiped my mouth with the back of my hand, and envisioned Crazy Tom cutting Slim open with his bowie knife, right there in the clubhouse, in front of all the other brothers. But nothing happened.

"Want me to fuck him up?" Mr. Happy waited for my cue, his eyes hungry for action.

A pall of apprehension hung over the party. This wasn't like watching football on television with teams no one knew or cared about. Here there were no replays, no commentaries, and no commercial breaks. Every fight had rules; *Outlaws* had rules, and none involved negotiations or huddles.

As I gave the command to attack, Duke, the Fugarwe's Boss, intervened. "He's ours," he said, and began to usher Slim into a back room.

"You either handle him or I will." It was an unwritten

rule in the biker world that each club disciplined its own. The punishment for insulting an Outlaw was two black eyes.

Adrenaline pumped through me like a drug. I wanted to pummel Slim myself, squeeze his fucking throat until his eyes popped. My whole body shook. The room spun. The caiman slept in his shallow pool, eyes wide open, mouth extended in a magnificent display of jagged teeth. Duke looked uneasy; blood drained from his face.

"We'll take care of it."

"If you don't, I'll be back next week to burn this fucking house down."

With that explosion, the party ended; lights flipped on, the music stopped. Brothers filtered into the alley. Broads headed for the exits. The scene consisted of littered shot glasses, half-full plastic cups, spilled liquid on the bar, pool sticks propped against the table, balls in some of the pockets, a buffet of uneaten food along the far walls. Upstairs a toilet flushed.

"You're a little over the top, Pete," Mountain said in a low voice.

My heart raced. "You're either with me or against me."

The next day, Joker called me. "We have a problem."

"I don't think we do."

"The Fugarwes are worried."

"So?" I leaned back in my plush leather chair and lit a cigarette.

"Slim's been handled internally," Joker said. "They drilled both of his eyes."

I didn't care about Slim's punishment. I cared about perception. *Big Pete* did not apologize.

"What do you want me to tell them?" Joker asked.

"Tell them to keep a fire extinguisher handy."

Joker sighed. "We have to call them and tell them it's okay."

"I'm not calling them," I said. "I'm ordering *you* to call them."

"I'm not doing it. You're the Boss."

Silence. Joker stuttered, "They won't listen to me."

Now he had my attention. I jammed my cigarette into the ashtray. *Interesting—they viewed him as Joker the Joke. This was huge.*

"We can't risk sending them into the arms of the Hells Angels. They want an apology," Joker continued.

I waited a day, let Joker sweat it out, then made my victory call to the Fugarwes.

"It's fine. It's enough."

And so, Duke resigned. He had no choice really; stalemate was not an option. He had to exit gracefully.

I often did my best thinking grocery shopping; I found it relaxing to roam each aisle and read ingredients. I marveled at pies that came in cans, ready-made graham cracker crusts, frozen spaghetti and tomato pastes that passed for sauce. I studied the shoppers, too; laser-focused, harried, most bought the same items every time, choosing familiar, safe, easy. Pieces of a televangelist's speech swirled in my head: "What we buy is a reflection of what we are, what we want, what we become. When we are born we are all given the opportunity of a life [and] time. We can save time, pass time, buy time, waste time, do time . . . even kill time. . . ."

When I tired of food items, I browsed toy sections, incredulous that square folks actually bought this shit. One day, I pressed the paw on a stuffed bulldog named Barney and it barked. I pretended to be a ventriloquist.

I wasn't remotely funny, but when my old lady found me sometime later in the dim hallway, pretending Barney spoke, she gushed I was "amazing," "wonderful," and should seriously consider a comedy career.

I replaced the toy on the shelf.

"You know you suck, right?" Mr. Happy rolled his eyes.

"You really *were* funny." Debbie smiled.

The Fugarwes held an annual pig roast on twenty acres of Cook County forest preserve. The event attracted biker and one-percenter clubs from all over the city and offered prime opportunity for Outlaws to gather intelligence, recruit prospects, and flex muscle. Under a large pavilion, broads flashed their tits in wet T-shirt contests, paraded on stage in thick makeup and chunky high heels, and, doused by hoses, wiggled shiny G-string asses to crowds of salivating wolves. Nearby, a beer truck flowed, replenishing kegs and pitchers until the air reeked of alcohol. Food stands surrounded the glazed skewed pig rotating on the open fire rotisserie style.

Yellow crime tape circled the Outlaws' section, where I sat in the middle waiting to be served. Probates guarded the perimeter, asking my permission each time for a civilian or other club to enter. By so doing, they perpetuated the illusion of my greatness, leaving the hundreds of spectators still waiting in line to gaze at me as if I were a showpiece, or an event.

"Boss," the probate barked, "citizen requests permission to enter."

I watched the faces in the crowd, their curiosity piqued, some slowly chewing their corn, others removing their sunglasses, cups of beer suspended in midair. Whispers, nudges, smiles from the broads; I felt like Tony Soprano, a wax figure about to come to life.

I nodded to the probate; the citizen entered and presented me with a plate of steaming food and pig parts. Junior brought me a bottle of Crown Royal and placed it on the picnic table.

A drunk stumbled in and tried to kiss my hand. With a slight nod of my head, Mr. Happy grabbed the stray *and* the probate and whisked them into the woods. When they returned a few minutes later, both had black eyes.

"Hey, Boss, ever heard of Reapers, Inc.?" Junior stood next to the picnic table.

"No."

Mr. Happy was already on it. "Boss wants to talk to you," he told two Reapers as he escorted them toward me.

"Who *are* you?" The two Reapers wore black vests prominently displaying a skeletal figure holding a red, white, and blue scythe.

"You said it was okay." The member squinted at me.

"I've never heard of you."

"Chef approved us."

"Corleone?"

"Yeah. And Chopper Johnny."

"You do realize there's *another* club called the Grim Reapers and their logo is nearly identical to yours?"

"Yeah, we perverted the name—you know, a little gallows humor?" He chuckled, but I wasn't laughing.

"Colors are sacred," I said, giving him a crash course in patches. "Bikers kill for these rockers. Identity is not a secret. We wear these on our vests like a neon sign."

"We were thinking of Murderers, Inc., but thought this one sounded better."

"What's your name?"

"Sergeant Sal Luciano."

"You're a *cop*?" Now I was really curious. "How about you and I meet later and hash this out?"

A hint of fear skittered across the sergeant's face.

"What the fuck, Corleone," I said later, pacing in my clubhouse. "I never approved Reapers, Inc."

"They wanted to run some charity thing."

"What charity thing?"

"I don't know; they wanted to raise money for some charity."

"That's a onetime deal. I never said they could fly colors in Chicago."

I met Sal at Corleone's restaurant in Melrose Park. The day was overcast, windy. Still, we sat outside.

"We're third-shifters." The sergeant grinned and ordered sausage and peppers.

"You're still cops."

"We have a different philosophy. We're about quality, not quantity."

"We have a different philosophy too," I said. "Outlaws and cops don't mix."

"We're just having fun."

I considered that it might be handy to know a few coppers.

"Tell you what: You can play around with the biker thing, but you can't show up at any of our events."

Sal nodded. "Fair enough."

A week later, a group of us Outlaws stumbled out of a bar in Chicago, drunk on margaritas, reckless, determined to sober up at the fashion show we were going to. We mounted our bikes, swerving in and out of traffic; *the last thing we needed was a DUI.* No one messed with us until we reached the suburbs: Cicero, Northlake, Elmwood Park, Lyons, Melrose Park.

"Shit." Wig-wags lit up the patrol car behind us. Sirens chirped and a voice boomed through the bullhorn, "What's going on?"

The cop pulled up next to me and rolled down his window. "Sal!"

The officer grinned. "You need an escort?"

What the fuck? His squad car shot ahead of us, sirens blaring down the freeway. We had to drive so fast to keep up with him that we missed our exit. He honked at us, pointed to a ramp *going the wrong way,* and promised to "be a lookout" for us while we flipped the bikes around into oncoming traffic.

"We thought *you* were chasing the *cops!*" a few onlookers remarked later.

And I could see how it might be confusing.

But after that first police escort, we took advantage of any public misperception, and Melrose Park, third shift, became a sanctuary where we could essentially do whatever we wanted. We could count on Sal and his third-shift crew. More often than not he showed up at whatever bar we were at, dressed in full uniform, ready to give us his blessing.

"You're not getting in trouble for this shit, are you?" I said.

"We're just having fun." Sal laughed.

But a newspaper warned that the officers were "treading on dangerous terrain":

> "Members of a Melrose Park motorcycle club called Reapers Inc. look the part of rough-and-ready outlaw bikers. They ride Harley-Davidsons, sport tattoos, hold parties at their clubhouse, pose for photos with middle fingers extended. . . .
>
> "But to hear it from the club's president, the group in no way embraces the damn-the-rules lifestyle espoused by the likes of the Hells Angels and Outlaws—two of the largest and better-known "outlaw," or "1%-er," biker organizations that have been

repeatedly targeted by federal authorities for drug trafficking and other alleged gangland activities.

"After all, the Reapers club was founded by Melrose Park cops. . . .

" 'We're nothing but a bunch of guys that like to hang out . . . and ride together,' said a patrol officer in the west suburb. 'All we want to do is have a good time.' "

At least we had that in common. Still, neither of us forgot which team we were on. Word of the outlaw/cop alliance spread and soon other graveyard crews were participating. Nicky, a third-shift cop who worked Northlake, tossed me his keys one night while I drank with Mr. Happy and other Outlaws.

"Ever wanted to drive a squad car?" he asked. *Was he kidding?*

I climbed into the front seat, borrowed Nicky's checkerboard hat, instructed Mr. Happy to replace the police department's logo with the Outlaws' insignia, "Charlie," and sped off, waving to other cars and pedestrians.

"I think third shift should wear Outlaw support patches," Nicky announced one night as he drove me home. I was too intoxicated to respond, but the next day I made sure third shift, Northlake, received patches and T-shirts.

They thanked me by posting club photos on Facebook; the members' vests all read, "Support Your Local Outlaw."

At two in the morning, I sat alone in a sports bar bordering Northlake. A heavy weight bag swung from the ceiling and patrons took turns hitting it. After a while, the punches were resounding like buckshot in my ears. *Punch. Bang. Punch. Bang.* I called Nicky.

"What's up?" he said when he arrived at the bar, dressed in uniform, looking weary.

"You hear that?"

Nicky nodded.

"Give me your gun." I pointed to his waistband.

"Now hold on, Pete." Nicky blocked my hand.

"I want to blow his fucking head off." I twisted the napkin under my shot glass.

"How about we take a ride?"

Nicky tossed me the keys to his squad car. And in my inebriated, strung-out condition I drove us to the deserted police firing range. Floodlights glowed over the dark silhouetted figures of torsos and heads on a rope with bull's-eyes for faces.

Nicky gave me his pistol.

I didn't bother with earplugs. I just aimed and fired over and over until his gun clicked.

Several weeks later, a SWAT team pulled me over as I rode near Stone Park. Sirens chirped. Streetlights flickered. It was one o'clock in the morning. I slowed, lowered the kickstand, shut off my bike.

"You don't have to do that," the officer pulled alongside me. "I just wanted to introduce myself." He held out his hand. *Introduce himself? What the fuck?*

"What's this all about?"

"You're Big Pete, right?"

"Am I in trouble?"

"No." The officer chuckled. "I just wanted to say hello."

"I'm not a prize pig."

"We're just curious."

"You realize we're not on the same side, right?" *We were never going to be friends.* I made a distinction between "good cops" and "cops that were good *for* us."

But when the officer was killed the following week in a bike wreck, I attended his funeral. The service was flooded with reporters. But while it was advantageous to have cops and reporters sympathetic to the Outlaws, it wasn't something I wanted broadcast.

"Lets just keep this between us, okay?" I said to one reporter.

But he didn't; instead his article highlighted the public's "fascination" with bikers and the "striking similarities" between us "misunderstood Robin Hoods" and "true believer" cops.

"People hear 'club' and think 'gang,'" one Wild Pig cop/member explained in the article, the difference between ninety-nine-percenter and one-percenter clubs. "We have rules of law; gangsters have *codes.*"

"A *gang,* which we most definitely are *not,* acts territorial or confrontational, uses profanity, vulgarity and antisocial messages on their cuts [jackets], bikes, Web sites. Gangs openly display/carry weapons in public and hang out with other like-minded individuals. They gravitate to brotherhood, attend functions, promote charities, and support gang activities, because they feel socially isolated from the public at large and have a human *need* for acceptance."

I could see how we were different.

Familiar dread cramped my lungs.

"I'm taking off for a while," I told friends, and hid in my bedroom for days, curtains drawn, dark shadows moving across the walls. Sometimes I needed to detach, disconnect, cross into a portal and flick a switch. A morose quiet engulfed me. I dozed on and off. My answering machine blinked at me like an angry red eye. Then Butch tapped at my window. He wore his embroidered black dress shirt.

"Hey, Pete," his voice exploded in my ear. *Tap. Tap. Tap.* "Pete? I'm dead. I'm *deeeeead* . . . I'm free. I'm finally free."

I sat bolt upright in bed, my heart racing. Room empty. Rain spit at the window.

My hand shook as I depressed the message button expecting to hear Butch's voice. Strangely, days before, he had left a message on my house phone; I'd recognized his caller ID. I never answered him. Now, the machine crackled. I hit rewind, hoping to hear his voice. Nothing.

"Debbie!" Panic took hold. She appeared in the doorway. "Did you erase Butch's message?"

She shook her head. "What message?"

Santa organized Butch's funeral and held the reception in an abandoned hotel because "it was cheap" and he "got a deal." Inside, the empty ballroom had a muggy, locker-wet smell. Sweat compounded the stickiness. The place was being remodeled. White tarps draped over built-in bars and stools. Mirrors circled the room, and a rickety chandelier dropped from the low ceiling. I half expected Butch to appear, not in a bloody, gory way but chuckling through the hollow corridors and tapping on the bullet-riddled glass.

Two strippers approached; one had a missing front tooth, the other an open sore on her right breast that resembled a bite mark. Debbie sat next to me, held my hand, suppressed a laugh as one stripper cut into my thigh with her butt bone and draped an arm around my neck.

"Get the fuck off me."

"We were told we needed to make you feel better," Santa apologized. "I know how much Butch meant to you." His wife blinked at Debbie; she had the face of a catcher's mitt.

"I told you he couldn't be trusted," Debbie whispered.

18

KARATE G-MAN

Mr. Happy's clientele was vintage Cicero and included regulars like the Large Guy, high-ranking gangbangers, Outlaw Bosses, and frequently junkies and whores.

"I see the Feds are still here." I motioned to the white van parked across the street at the Chevron station.

Mr. Happy smirked and finished selling a large-screen television to a clean-cut chatterbox who suspiciously resembled a cop.

"Where did *he* come from?" I lit a cigarette. *I never purchased anything but meat from Mr. Happy's shop. Food, at least, could be consumed and contained no traceable serial numbers.*

"He was driving by and saw my poster in the window."

"You're kidding, right?"

The "poster," which advertised an MMA competition involving Mr. Happy's son, was the size of a sheet of paper. Cars whizzed by on Cicero and Roosevelt. No driver stopped on purpose much less slowed down to register a tiny-printed ad.

"What did he want?"

"He knows the dojo sponsoring my kid's fight."

I'm sure he does. I'm sure the Feds briefed him thoroughly on Mr. Happy's son and the MMA studio situated across the street from the police station, the same department the Feds regularly monitored from a trailer they parked in the lot.

"I'll introduce you next time."

"No thanks," I said.

But the following week Artie, a Berwyn cop, lingered in the back room, sucking down Marlboro Reds. I watched him, hidden in plain sight, as he smoked one after another, his eyes watery, his face puffy and slick. Afternoon shadows played across rows and rows of crates in the back room.

I asked Artie for a cigarette: a "cowboy killer." He wore baggy clothes, *perfect for hidden wires.*

"Yeah, sure." Artie fumbled for one and handed it to me, but never offered me a light.

"I don't trust him," I said to Mr. Happy. "Who smokes and doesn't carry a lighter."

"You don't trust anyone."

"I don't like him."

"He's harmless."

"He never shuts up."

I tossed the unlit cigarette into the trash. "Stay away from him," I said. "I mean it."

●   ●   ●

That night I read my favorite parts of *The Godfather* again. And when I got to the scene about Michael wanting to kill the police captain I underlined the passage . . . specifically the unwritten rule that mobsters didn't kill cops . . . *unless they crossed the line.*

"What if I feed him misinformation?" Mr. Happy said as he finished his can of Red Bull.

"You're not the fucking CIA."

Mr. Happy huddled regularly with Artie, whose laugh made me cringe. I never asked about their conversations, but I did continue to watch Artie, the way a child might study a scorpion trapped behind glass. His father was a made man in the Chicago Outfit. Artie's default was to join the police department.

I stopped having lunch with Mr. Happy.

"I don't think Karate G-Man is a Fed," he said during one of my last visits.

"Why is that?"

"We hung out together last night, talked until six in the morning."

That would certainly convince me.

When the call came from the Feds a few weeks later I wasn't surprised.

"We have a search warrant for your clubhouse and would rather not break down the front door." The Fed recited the signboard I had laminated requesting that the cops "call first" before destroying property.

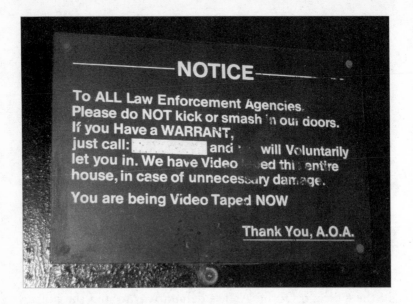

Sign leading into the North Side clubhouse

My hands stilled on my laptop keyboard as I sunk into my large living room sofa.

"I understand." I felt a little numb as I hung up and immediately dialed a few cohorts, sounding like Paul Revere: "The Feds are coming."

"They're already here," Big Dog said. Papers shuffled in the background.

"What's happening?"

"I never turned the fucking machines on."

I called Ray Rayner next.

"We never plugged them into the wall." For once, I found his stupidity a relief.

With heart pounding, I orchestrated the various support clubs to circulate and discard their video gambling machines.

Sweet Home Chicago Party, Southside Clubhouse; Pete (center), Mr. Happy (right).

Pete and Brutus relaxing in the backyard.

50th birthday cake given to Pete by Coyote and his crew.

At Chicago Northside clubhouse, toasting the brothers in prison. Featured in the rear is Ray Rainer, Maurice, Butch #2, and The Hound.

Pete partying with Jaws 1%er GBNF "Gone But Not Forgotten."

Pete and Gypse at Freedom Blast Party. Featured behind Pete: memorial plaque. Every chapter pays tombstone tax of $100.

Pete with Mr. Happy on their way to Daytona Bike Week.

Bikes at Sweet Home Chicago.

First COC fundraiser; Pete, Gypse, and Gabby.

Freedom Blast Party, Northside (July).

Run at Alton Illinois Chapter clubhouse for the River Run.

Pete talking to a Bandido.

Pete and Debbie in the Outlaws' clubhouse.

Pete at home.

Pete's "Ray Ban" look.

•   •   •

"Do I need to worry?" Debbie paled on the couch.

"It's not illegal to *own* machines," I assured her. "They have to prove I'm *paying out*."

Flustered, I left for the North Side and waved to the Feds parked askew at the curb. Some followed me into my office, grabbed an edge of couch or hugged the wall. I sat on my throne, perfectly aligned with the gold statute of Caesar's head.

"How can I help?"

One whipped out a recorder and depressed the red button. "What do you know about the Double-O Alliance?"*

Nothing I was willing to share.

A news report later implicated "The Large Guy," head of the Chicago Mafia's video gambling rackets, and his enforcer, "Goldberg the Jew" (aka Mr. Happy), a "member of the Outlaws Motorcycle Gang and [The Large Guy's] primary fence for stolen merchandise."

Amusements, Inc., The Large Guy's business, was referred to as a "criminal enterprise operating in and around Cicero" and responsible for distributing machines to local bars and restaurants."

"These machines," a reporter explained, "allowed customers to deposit money in return for virtual credits (legal so long as used for amusement only) which they redeemed for cash. The devices were modified to track money coming in and being paid out, so that the establishment owners and the enterprise could each take a cut of the profits."

---

* The Chicago Outfit and Outlaws

"What do you know about his competitor, C&S Amusements?" the Fed pressed.

Nothing I was willing to share.

C&S Amusements, Inc., undercut The Large Guy's profits, offering greater percentages and supplying machines to a series of eateries and taverns that "belonged" to The Large Guy. After fair warning to "stay the fuck away" from Cicero, The Large Guy* dispatched his enforcers with a message for his competitor: a firebomb.

"You're the number two regional vice president of the Chicagoland chapters," the Fed read me my resume. "We're pretty sure you know things." He glared at me, his eyes like blue cut glass.

"Do I need a lawyer?"

"That's entirely up to you."

"Well, am I under arrest?"

"Not yet." He smiled.

Wind blew through the open door, dumped garbage on the kitchen tiles, papers scattered like confetti. Foam chunks puffed from the couch. Bladed shadows of a ceiling fan clicked above us. I knew the Feds would find nothing. I never installed machines in my *own* clubhouse. The place was eerily empty, resembled gutted rooms in an abandoned warehouse.

"Then what do you want?"

---

* The Large Guy, Michael Sarno, was convicted in 2010 and sentenced to twenty-five years in prison. Eventually Mr. Happy was also indicted and received sixty years; six others, including a former Berwyn police officer, were indicted on charges of racketeering and conspiracy.

"Help."

"What kind of help?"

"We need information."

A slow smile spread across my face. "You didn't just ask me to be a rat, right?"

"People are freaked out," I said to Debbie later. "We need to make some appearances. We need to tell them everything is going to be fine, business as usual."

Debbie nodded. That's what I loved about her. She never asked for details, never asked questions. She just accepted that we would spend the rest of the night riding down dangerous streets, knocking on clubhouse doors, giving brief speeches (as any leader with a nation in peril would) that everything was going to be fine, that everything *was* fine, we were all fine.

"You sure?"

No—we were so fucked. The Feds confiscated the Christmas cards; I'd once made a big deal about the club never throwing any of them away. But the cards contained every member's address.

Truth was, I thought about prison all the time, about inadvertently becoming King of Nothing, like Dr. Seuss's *Yertle the Turtle,* with a stone for a throne overlooking a pond. Taco, the International Boss of the Outlaws, ruled a prison empire. He controlled things from his solitary cell, promised Ray Rayner and Santa status "beyond just Boss of an Outlaw chapter," just as soon as he "got out of here." They became his enforcers, his Luca Brasis, though I was pretty confident neither had actually read *The Godfather*. And I was pretty positive Taco, who was serving a double life sentence plus thirty-five years for murder and RICO convictions, was never being released.

"Peter, Peter." Backlash grinned. "You're learning fast."

And though Taco had been officially "gone" since 1997, he was still a presence, like a lingering ghost. Brothers who never knew him loyally visited him, campaigning for his freedom, reveling in his stories from "back in the day" when he was a *real* gangster. He personified the price Outlaws paid to *be* Outlaws. He'd had a clubhouse like a fortress and once tossed a citizen off a balcony in Daytona Beach after he chipped an Outlaw's tooth.

Taco wrote me letters, encouraged me to "enter his circle." But his trustees included Ray Rayner and Santa, and I knew the truth about them. My resistance was no deterrence to Taco. He sent Debbie a purse.

19

GOD FORGIVES, OUTLAWS DON'T

"We need an emergency meeting." Santa sounded frantic. I cupped the phone to my ear as I watched Jerry Springer slide down a stripper pole and wave to his audience. To the chant of "Jer-ry! Jer-ry!" he shook hands with spectators in the front row.

"Got a call from a guy in Milwaukee," Santa said.

"You mean *Jack?*" *The Boss?*

A producer flashed a title card: "Show may contain inappropriate content." Security waited in the wings, looking like thugs from the Outfit. The audience settled down as Jerry greeted his first guest, a broad in a tight miniskirt and midriff blouse. She wheelchaired onstage, waved to the crowd, and proudly displayed the two nubs she called "legs."

"Ony was on *Gangland,*" Santa continued. "He said he was Out Bad with the Outlaws but was still allowed to keep his tattoos and all his property."

This was serious. He could be killed for that kind of lie. Any Outlaw "out bad" never got to keep his property. Jerry ran through the audience with a chain saw; between buzzes he shouted, "She's *happy* she cut off her legs."

I stepped into the lobby so I could hear. "Tell Jack I'll handle this."

"Why you watch that shit?" Mr. Happy laughed. "Bunch of freaks wanting attention. You could see that *here*."

I called Ony. "Meet me tomorrow morning at IHOP. Don't be late."

I arrived alone, an hour early so I would always have the advantage fully expecting Ony to pull a shine move and, in gangbanger fashion, try to pop me execution style. It would have been a desperate move on his part, knowing he had few choices left. I grabbed a seat by the window in full view of the nearly empty parking lot and flipped through the program guide on the TV for upcoming Springer episodes. Next week's episode featured a "Transsexual Takedown."

Ony pulled up at the agreed-upon time, waited a few minutes before shutting off his engine. He walked slowly toward the entrance, peering behind him, hands shoved into his front pockets. He paced, smoked a cigarette, crushed the ash with his boot, and sat for a few minutes on the bench.

I glanced at my watch; twenty minutes had passed. *Jesus, Ony, I don't have all day.*

"I've always respected you," he said as he slid across from me at last, removed his sunglasses, and clasped his hands in front of him. "You always treat people fair." He ordered a stack of blueberry shortcakes. His voice cracked.

"Don't kiss my ass," I cut him off. "This is a onetime deal. Take it or leave it; but if you leave it you'll be looking over

THE LAST CHICAGO BOSS

your shoulder for the rest of your life." A brother out bad who doesn't cover up his tattoos can expect a trip to the hospital.

"What do I have to do?"

"Date your tattoos."

"Date my . . ."

"This is nonnegotiable," I said. "I'll put you out good, but you have to date them."

Ony's breakfast arrived, and he poured syrup on top of the whipped cream. "Okay. . . ."

"You're going to put my birth date on your tattoos—4/25/2007." *No one had ever proposed something like this before. But it was the only way I could think of to ensure Ony's safety. At least this way he had a fighting chance. Brothers might still help him if he was "out good."*

Ony nodded; he looked relieved. His whole face relaxed. He shoveled a large bite into his mouth. Syrup dribbled onto his chin.

"You're a gentleman, gangster."

"I try to be at least fifty percent good."

That's why I practiced balance; for every evil act committed, it was critical that I did something good (Respect+Fairness−Ruthlessness=Happiness). So when Rose showed up like nightshade after parties, dressed in fitted jeans, stiletto heels, and impeccably sprayed hair, reeking of desperation, it was difficult to be cruel.

"Hi." She waved her perfectly manicured nails. I noticed things like fingers and toes. Extremities reflected a person's insides: If nails were cracked, chipped, or fungus-black, I knew the person was mostly dead.

Rose interrupted my conversation with Bastardo and unwittingly broke Club Rule #36: A citizen never interrupts when Outlaws are speaking. And so began "The Dilemma with Rose."

Outlaw, Judas, immediately pounced, his hot breath in her face, voice booming, "Get the fuck out, skank." Rose's expression snapped. Dark lines smudged the creases of her eyes, a stray, fake lash stuck to her cheek. Her lips parted, quivered, and she began to cry.

I watched her shake, and something inside me snapped. I pulled Judas aside. "Why'd you have to make her cry?"

"She interrupted you."

"Be ruthless and thoughtless. Be an enforcer Outlaw," I said. "But don't abuse the power. Don't make girls cry."

He looked dumbfounded.

"You're just an ass," I elaborated. "Be a badass."

But not even I could be a badass all the time. Two years (or two football seasons) maximum—no matter the business: drug dealing, escort service—the Feds typically investigated criminal activity for eighteen months before initiating a raid. Unless, of course, murder was involved—then the Feds entered sooner.

With drugs, I didn't really think about fallout; instead the image of Frank, hauled away in shackles, destined to live out his remaining years captive in a cold cell, sobered me. *It could happen to me. Luck runs out. Time runs out. What once seemed so solid can slip away without warning. And one day you're fixated on cockroaches surrounded by concrete. Life over.*

After twenty-two months in the escort business, I hunted for a buyer: "I'm selling the little black book." Pages and pages of names, services, numbers. *Human beings.* That detail bothered the margins of my conscience just a little. Nonetheless, I asked a substantial sum for the book.

"You don't put a gun to the girls' heads." Mr. Happy facilitated the matches, ran the operation like a bookie.

True, but maybe it was the same thing in the end. These broads had kids they supported. If I shut down the operation, what would happen to them? Still, my decision to end my involvement impacted broads who had dedicated two years of good service. They had a limited shelf life, like quarterbacks: old at thirty.

Angel managed the girls for me. It wasn't fair to just *leave* her: "Thanks for the business, goodbye." *Who does that?* Sociopaths maybe, but I wasn't *that* kind of criminal.

I followed a felonious code of ethics—"Honor among thieves"—and strived to leave a person better off than when I first found them. Criminals didn't have to be assholes; it was important to balance the good deeds with the bad. In her mid-thirties, Angel had no skills; she couldn't compete with the hard bodies of twenty-year-olds.

"There's nothing left for me." She blew her nose. "I'm a used-up whore."

"Nonsense, you're just retired," I said. "You need an investor."

"For what?"

"Your 401k plan."

I conceived of Enchanted Luna, a tarot "mystic" shop owned and operated by Angel and staffed by former whores and strippers. My friend owned space in Berwyn Township, a densely populated Hispanic suburb in Cook County.

"Mexicans love spiritual shit," I assured Angel. "Guadalupe, candles, readings. You could make a killing."

I "donated" a few glass jewelry cases to the shop and designed business cards for Angel that listed her as "Proprietor."

I popped in frequently to check out my investment.

"Why aren't you open?"

"I'm experimenting with hours." Angel yawned. It was two o'clock in the afternoon and the shop was locked.

"Customers aren't going to drop in after dark," I said. "You're not a whore anymore—you're reading people's fortunes. If you're closed you can't make money."

"I'm not sure this is really my thing—you know, sitting for hours and hours waiting to service people."

"Are you disappointed she closed the shop?" Debbie asked me after a couple of months.

"I gave her an opportunity. It's up to her to take it. I did my good deed."

Angel was good for my conscience. And ultimately she got what she wanted: a welfare check. She found the poor sperm donor—a cop, no less—online, married and divorced him within a few months, and happily entered the system.

"It's important to know what you are in this world," I said to Debbie. "That way you're never disappointed."

• • •

One blustery morning in June, I sat in my office, cracked my knuckles, and listened to the phone ring, again and again. *Leave a message. If I don't pick up the first time, don't keep calling.* I finally snatched the receiver.

"Uh . . . okay . . ." *Click.*

The phone rang again. I placed the caller on hold and piped in compositions by Rossini, Bellini, Verdi, and Puccini. I liked opera; someone always got stabbed. In college, I once interned for an attorney who said classical music soothed his clients. Pink office walls probably had the same effect.

After another hour of many ignored calls, I finally picked up, ready to explode.

"I'm getting a fortune." Pinkie, one of the whores who'd worked for me, sounded breathless on the other end.

We sat at a small table in the corner of the bar she now worked. Harsh daylight highlighted her pale, sunken cheeks, bottle-bleached curls, and skimpy tank. Creases framed sparkling ice blue eyes. Though she spoke, I heard only chatter. Key words pinged in my head: "bike wreck"; "settlement"; "personal injury lawsuit"; "torn rotator cuff."

"Be careful not to blow the money." My mouth felt dry.

"I want to start a business." She reeked of alcohol. "But I need a partner."

"What kind of business?" My fingers tingled at the sound of money.

"Crystals."

She elaborated with a cloth napkin. "Bandannas decorated with Swarovski crystals."

●   ●   ●

I hired a company to produce the merchandise, expanded the business to include T-shirts, and arranged for Pinkie to participate in trade shows to sell and market the products.

"Why am I fielding calls for orders?" I barked at Pinkie later. I heard glasses clinking in the background.

She slurred her words. "I have a day job, you know."

Yeah, me too.

"This isn't working out so well," I said. "No one's going to waste a hundred bucks on fancy bandannas that could blow off their skull at high speed."

20

THE FALL

After the bandanna-Swarovski crystal debacle, I turned my marketing attention to the COC. And in time, I designed patches ("Confederation of Clubs") for members, set up run sheets, planned an all-club ride, and established a scholarship fund for any person going to school, be it trade school, college, or junior college. *After all, the Hells Angels annually donated money to Toys for Tots—why shouldn't the COC give to charitable causes?*

"It's not like we don't have a heart." I lit my fifth cigarette in an hour.

"I love hearing you speak." Gypse, my vice chairman and a member of Brothers Rising, shook my hand at the end of a presentation. He choked up, said he had ridden two hours "for the poetry." The high was like a drug, gazing into a crowd of hundreds as I spoke—unscripted, "from the heart," sometimes four hours at a stretch with no breaks.

"Good speech, Boss." Mr. Happy sucked back cans of Red Bull as he drove me home. Meetings began at noon, and by the time they ended and attendees said their goodbyes it was nearly dark. Fleetingly, I wondered if politicians experienced this same combination of exhilaration and fatigue.

I recovered in my bedroom. Debbie brought me steaming bowls of chicken soup. I stacked soggy carrot slivers along the edges. My computer screen lit up with Civilization III, the strategy video game that involved building an empire from the ground up. The objectives were to construct and improve cities, train military and nonmilitary units, improve terrain, research technologies, and make war (or peace) with neighboring civilizations.

I wanted to build an MC world.

But first, I had to set up a "regime," (just like Michael Corleone did in *The Godfather*), a Spanish coalition to encompass the ten Chicago Hispanic clubs, who preferred to be called "associations" so that they could circumvent motorcycle club rules. There were too many to monitor; I needed help.

I nominated Coyote, the wiry Boss of Twisted Image, to "get the clubs together," and instructed him, "Tell them Big Pete wants to meet."

In a different world Coyote would have been director of marketing; he scheduled several gatherings with the various clubs, served up decent food, and before ever introducing me created buzz about "a legend": "Big Pete wants to work with you"; "Big Pete wants to form an alliance"; "You'll be working with Big Pete."

"Big Pete" recruited an entourage to perpetuate this

larger-than-life persona. Bodyguards held car doors open for me, walked two paces behind as a sign of respect. Crowds formed along busy sidewalks, and strangers tittered, "That's him—that's Big Pete." But soon, the show got a little ridiculous and I grew concerned that my fake entourage might actually telegraph my movements to any watchful Feds.

I cut back. This was, after all, my show, and it wasn't real. I was perpetuating an illusion. Meanwhile, Coyote convinced the ten Hispanic clubs to pledge their allegiance to the Outlaws. They became part of my phantom army and made regular appearances at Outlaw clubhouses, just in case the Angels had spies. I wanted them to see we were *huge*.

In many ways I felt forced to fight the Angels without the Outlaws. Santa's "hands off" policy made it nearly impossible to rally reliable soldiers. The COC became my proxy.

With Coyote's help, I expanded. More and more clubs wanted to join. I recruited over six hundred members, a small army.

Coyote arranged the meetings, ordering members to show up by dusk. He rattled off addresses of holes in the wall, dive bars frequented by shines and the Ole Skool Road Playerz. It was clear I didn't belong, but by the time I made my entrance, Coyote had deified me into some kind of god. I was ushered onto a makeshift stage and given a beer—and silent, undivided attention.

"Why do they call you The Professor?" I asked the Boss of the Ole Skool Road Playerz.

He wore a leather cowboy hat, tinted gold sunglasses,

leather knuckle gloves, a cropped beard, and a leather vest embroidered with the club's motto, "We do not go along to get along."

"I teach law classes at a community college."

"Are you a lawyer?" He could've passed for one, and it might be handy to have someone familiar with statutes of limitations.

"No." The Professor chuckled. He removed his glasses, wiped a lens on his vest. "I lead political debates."

I did too. We were kindred spirits.

"You want to slap 'Support your Local Outlaw' patches on *shines*' vests?" Bastardo was having trouble processing my proposal, as if he thought that somehow I didn't realize the significance of the gesture . . . that shines *would actually have to support the Outlaws.*

"Yes," I said.

"You do realize The Outlaws are mostly white supremacists?"

"We don't want shines in our clubhouse," Santa put his foot down. I was certain he never quite realized how ridiculous he sounded.

"They'll be part of the COC."

"I don't care."

"We're fighting discrimination against patch-holders." I said, pointing out the obvious.

"I get that. But not *them*."

"Look here, we can't be a club about nondiscrimination and discriminate."

"We'll just have to make an exception."

"What are we doing here?"

Santa whined, "If we let shines into the COC, then they'll want to come to the clubhouses and to the parties and . . ."

I shook my head. "This isn't about *color*, it's about money."

Santa still didn't get it.

"Who do you think makes up our juries?" I asked him. "The Outlaws need allies. At some point they'll need to defend against allegations of hate crimes."

"So you want to *buy* their support?"

"I wouldn't put it that way."

"What way then?"

"It's a two-way street. We can help each other."

But not every shine appreciated my concept of solidarity. Shortly after distributing the support patches to the Ole Skool Road Playerz, I met resistance one night as I drove home from Church. The North Side clubhouse bordered several rough black neighborhoods, and my route took me through the edge of their turf. My wheels slid to a stop on a patch of ice at the intersection.

A cluster of shines huddled on the corner, their long coats flapping in the wind. The tallest of the group waved me down; he approached my car, flashed open his coat, and displayed his .22. A shot to the head or neck would probably have killed me. I could have gunned the engine, flattened the fucker right there on the pavement and left his remains for the street crawlers, but this was politics.

Better to send a message.

I retrieved my .40-caliber Glock from the armrest next

to me. *As one of the few who could still legally carry, I'm sure I surprised him.* My windows fogged from cold. The tall one traced a frosty circle with his finger and drew a line through the center. I shined my Maglite in his face. Threatening violence was always more powerful than pulling the trigger.

I rolled down the window and said, "There can only be one rooster in the henhouse. Cock-a-doodle-do."

"I don't think he got the message," Bastardo said as he woke me up from a dead sleep the next morning.

"What's the matter?"

"Ghost paid me a visit."

Ghost was the head shine of Chicago's shine club, the Wheels of Soul.

"We have a problem. The Hell's Lovers and Wheels of Soul stole the Ole Skool Road Playerz' vests last night."

"What happened?" I called "The Professor."

"They took our patches."

I could tell from his tone that he didn't understand the seriousness of the act. "Why did you *let* them?"

"We were outnumbered." He said it matter-of-factly, as if we were discussing his wallet being stolen. But these weren't just his club's patches, because frankly I wouldn't have cared if those had been stolen: These were *Outlaw support patches*—Outlaw support patches I had given to shines.

"I have to get them *back*," I told Debbie.

"How are you going to manage that?" she asked.

I remembered a curious exchange a year earlier at an NCOM convention in Charlotte, North Carolina, when the vice president of the Wheels of Soul gave me his number.

"In case you ever need to call Preacher Mon," he said, grinning.

Never could I have imagined needing a shine for anything, but I'd kept his contact information nonetheless.

I called in my favor.

"I've got a fucking problem," I said as I paced the confines of my room. "Your boys out here stole my property."

I told Preacher Mon the story.

He listened thoughtfully and said, "I'll get back to you."

"Don't forget me." When I hung up I felt a little lightheaded. *If the fucker didn't call me back . . . I was fucked, I was so fucked.* Colors were worth killing for . . . even dying for . . . *and if the Outlaws found out their patches were gone . . .*

Two hours later, my phone lit up with a Philadelphia area code.

"This is Dirty Harry," the National Boss of the Wheels of Soul introduced himself.

"Well, *Dirty Harry,* I'm the Regional Boss of the Chicago Outlaws. You're new to this city. You'll either be welcomed or obliterated." Stress made me sound a little like a *Star Trek* alien.

"What's the problem?"

"The *problem*"—I took a deep breath—"is that Wheels of Soul have Outlaw patches."

"Let me get back to you."

"Don't forget me."

Ghost called me next. "Do you know who I am?"

"Do you know who *I* am?" I could feel my face get hot.

"I'm friends with Mark from the jewelry store." Ghost said.

It took me a minute to register that his "Mark" was actually Mr. Happy.

"Well you're talking to Mark's boss."

Ghost coughed. Silence followed, and for a minute I actually thought he had hung up.

"Hey man, I'm sorry, I didn't realize you were him. *The* Big Pete."

"Shut up. I want my property back."

"Where do you want to meet and who are you bringing with you?

"No one. Meet me at noon in the middle of the parking lot of the Illinois Harley."

It felt like a high noon showdown in some weird spaghetti western. I arrived early, parked askew in the middle of the empty lot, and waited for Ghost. He pulled up a few minutes later in his Escalade with an entourage of six thugs.

"I've got your shit."

"I know." I popped open the trunk. "Throw the vests in there."

Ghost looked a little bewildered. "That's it?"

"I'm not shaking hands."

"You didn't bring anyone with you?"

"What for?"

Ghost snapped his fingers, and his puppets tossed the vests in my trunk.

I drove to the Ole Skool Road Playerz' clubhouse. "No

one gives up his patches," I said to The Professor. "You should be willing to die for them."

He nodded, and his oversized glasses slid down the bridge of his nose.

"You want your patches back?"

"Definitely."

"It'll cost you."

"How much?"

"Two thousand dollars."

He nodded. "Sounds reasonable."

"I've got them in the trunk."

"My patches are in the trunk of your Cadillac?"

I popped open the trunk to show him. "Get the money."

"I will." The Professor grinned.

"Meet me in the middle of the parking lot of the Illinois Harley, tomorrow, noon."

For the second time in two days I arrived early to an empty parking lot and waited for shines.

"I've got the money," The Professor said as he rode up with his entourage of six gangsters.

"I know."

"You want to count it?"

"Definitely." I took my time—licked my fingers and made a production of separating each bill. And then handed him $1,000 back.

"I don't understand."

"If you lose these patches again, it will cost you ten thousand bucks to get them back." The more pebbles I skipped across the still pond, the wider the ripples.

• • •

Santa called a few days later to complain, "Ray Rayner says you're sanctioning everybody."

I bristled. "First of all, I never *sanction* any club." The idea that I accepted *any* club for the *club's* sake was dangerous.

"That's what Ray Rayner is saying."

"So."

"What do you mean 'so'?" Santa sounded like he dropped a screwdriver on the concrete.

"S. O."

"Why are you encouraging all of these clubs to form?"

"Let me pose this scenario to you," It was easier if I thought of him as a bigheaded child. "Five guys walk into a clubhouse and ask permission to become a club. I say no. They leave. The tough guy in the group pauses outside and mumbles under his breath, "Fuck him. Why do we have to do what he says? Let's start our own anyway.'"

Santa said nothing.

"Is Ray Rayner going to hunt this new club down and demand accountability? Will *you*?"

Again nothing.

"No. *I* will. If I can even find them," I broke the silence.

All I heard was breathing.

"Why not make them our friends? Most of these idiots won't even be around in two years. They'll wither on the vine, disappear, poof, gone. Problem solved."

"Okay, I see your point."

"Bye."

•   •   •

It was a kind of game for me: Random prospective groups approached me regularly to ask my approval to form a new club.

"A lot goes into this," I told one group of hopefuls as I invited them to the clubhouse, instructing them to bring their members and all of their paraphernalia.

We didn't meet in my office—that was reserved for invited guests. Instead I sat in the center of the room and made them all stand in a semicircle.

"Who do we have?" There were five of them, including the clearly marked sergeant at arms, president, and vice president.

"So you're the sergeant at arms?"

The man stepped forward, his chest as wide as a beam. "That's right."

"You do understand you're the first one shot?"

As if I had popped him with a pin, the man instantly deflated.

"And you're the president?" I pointed to the next man in line, who had an embroidered "President" patch on his vest.

"Yes."

"Well, you're the second one to get shot."

This man, too, paled, shifted uncomfortably, and had no response.

I continued. "You're the vice president?"

"Yes."

"You'll be running away and take a bullet in the back."

They stared at me dumbfounded.

"Doesn't everyone know who you are?"

Again silence.

"Look here, why would you broadcast your titles? A patch that identifies your rank makes you a moving target."

The shine clubs were not my only challenge. My vision for the COC was to eliminate rivalry altogether, to create an army of thirty-seven loyal clubs and all their soldiers, who, though once autonomous, would now consider me their leader.

"I'm not taking orders from a woman," a member of the Hillbillies, a Polish club, complained at the next COC meeting after one of its particularly entrepreneurial female members splintered off and formed a mixed male/female social club.

I made my Big Mistake after eight members disbanded suddenly from the Hillbillies and formed their own club, Legacy, multiplying like octopi. Though they initially pledged their allegiance to the Outlaws, they soon became rogues, implementing their own rules, missing Outlaw parties and runs, arriving late to charity events.

"They're blackballing Sokol."

"Maybe they don't understand what a 'support club' does. After all, they don't speak much English. . . ."

"I don't give a fuck if they speak purple." I summoned Legacy's leader, Doc, and his eight minions to my office in the North Side clubhouse.

"You don't get to make up your own rules." Doc's face

and neck bloomed pink. He stood, arms crossed, neck craned so he could look me in the eye. I worried my large fan might blow him to the back of the room. The more I ranted, the more Doc quivered, the more his minions sweated. When I started to smash appliances, I knew I had driven home my point.

Doc's shoulders shook; his eyes filled with tears. His reaction caught me off guard. No leader had ever *cried* before.

"He's gone," Bastardo reported to me a week later.

"What do you mean *gone*?"

"Doc returned to Poland."

This news made me uneasy. No leader was ever "gone" *gone*. He regrouped, recalculated. I had emasculated Doc before his peers, and quite possibly committed a tactical error. After all, I couldn't afford to alienate *any* club in Chicago.

I paid Legacy a visit. Its clubhouse was situated in a converted and mostly empty warehouse.

"He's gone," Doc's replacement confirmed. And I noticed that his eight minions had disappeared with him.

"Is he coming *back*?"

The replacement shrugged and said, "No speak English."

I called Angel. "They're up to something. I need intel."

"How many girls?"

"At least five. I need to find out what Legacy is up to."

While the broads worked their way into Legacy's inner

circle as escorts, I fielded a bigger problem: "Shep, The Warrior, just got out of prison," Bastardo advised. "He wants his old job back."

He had been an Outlaw during the heyday, and part of the bombings. "He's from Gary, Indiana, the boil on the armpit of Chicago," I said.

"Well, he just gave the Rebel Knights* permission to wear the one-percenter diamond patch on their vests."

Technically, the COC boasted a zero discrimination policy, *except* that cops were not allowed. The Rebel Knights had two chapters in Chicago and a lone clubhouse in the middle of a cornfield in Indiana, close to Gary and The Warrior's turf. They had four cops as members, including their Boss, a sergeant in charge of the organized crime division of the Chicago Police Department.

"Just because the Rebel Knights are grandfathered into the COC doesn't give them the right to wear the diamond."

"They asked me"—The Warrior wiped his hands on a greasy towel as he stepped back to admire his bike's latest upgrades—"and I cleared it with Santa."

That explained a lot.

"Isn't that Mr. Happy's bike?"

"I'm holding it for him."

"He needs to sell it. He needs the money for his defense."

He really needed it for his appeal; no one ever won at trial.

"You can *buy* it from him."

---

* The club evolved into the Blue Knights, an all-cop club.

"How much does he want?"

"Eleven thousand dollars."

The Warrior laughed. "I put a few thousand into the repairs. The bike's only worth five thousand."

"He wants eleven thousand."

We compromised; The Warrior gave me $7,500 and promised to "make up the difference" by introducing me to his dealer Roy Boy.*

Roy Boy's tattoo shop was located on a deserted, charred street in Gary that gave me an idea of what neighborhoods in Beirut must look like: dilapidated buildings, strewn debris in the streets, spiderwebbed glass on the windows from shotgun blasts.

Roy Boy shook my hand; his were completely sleeved, with an illustrated skull and tufts of blond hair that skimmed his shoulders. His eyes had a yellow tint. Four caged tigers prowled his brick workspace; the lone white tiger skulked on a leash in the corner and yawned. A chain-link fence surrounded several black Bentleys with flat tires, pricey bikes worth at least $50,000.

"I need to move eight thousand South African gold Krugerrands."

It took me a minute to process the enormity of his request. Transporting seven hundred pounds of gold required a van, dollies, a forklift.

"Take a couple of days to put the operation together," I

---

* Aka Roy Cody Cooper

said. Roy stroked his white tiger's head, then replied, "Stay at one of my houses if you want." He tossed me the keys.

And over the next few days I orchestrated the logistics and salivated over the prospect of collecting *millions*. But when I reconnected with Roy, he was moaning on his couch, with a bloated stomach.

"Your liver's failing. You need to get to a hospital," I said.

"It's just constipation." Roy struggled to sit up. "We do this tomorrow."

I wasn't too sure.

Still, I returned the next day.

Roy's property had three padlocks and a dead bolt on the front door. His tigers, visible through the chipped windows, looked ravenous.

"He's in a coma," a nurse at the hospital advised.

Fuck! Not that I wanted to sound unsympathetic, but I had no idea where Roy hid the gold blocks.

"Guard his house," I instructed The Warrior.

The minute anyone in that neighborhood knew Roy Boy might not return, the raiding would begin. And the gold would be looted.

The hospital released Roy a week later, barely conscious. His private "nurse" sponged his lips with Jack Daniel's. Roy's eyes followed her tits as they bulged out of the uniform. Meanwhile, I mixed Roy's morphine with Sprite and gulped it down.

"It's over," I said to Debbie as I plopped into bed fully dressed in boots and vest. *Millions gone.*

Debbie left me a fresh banana on the nightstand, tip curled away from me just the way I liked.

Santa called me before the next COC meeting. "You're agitating the Rebel Knights."

" 'Agitating'?"

"They've offered to host the next National at their clubhouse in Gary. It's rumored you're being hostile."

" 'Hostile'?"

"Their leader suggested to The Warrior that he relieve you."

"Really?"

"Look, if we piss them off we'll just push the Rebel Knights into the arms of the Hells Angels."

"Their Boss is a fucking cop," I exploded. "You want to host the National at their clubhouse? It's a square in the middle of an empty field."

Silence. Papers were shuffled. Santa cleared his throat and asked, "does National know about this?"

"Maybe you should bring it up," I said. "Tell them The Warrior is proposing that the meeting be held at a cop's house."

Soon after, The Warrior was asked to "retire."

"There's a new Polish club," Angel reported to me. "They call themselves the Road Runners."

"Doc's?"

"Yes."

The revelation made me uneasy. *How many more rogue clubs existed?*

"Have you seen these Road Runners?" I asked when I reached out to the Boss of Legacy at his clubhouse. The place was dark inside; it looked like it had been condemned. A faint Clorox smell wafted through the vents in the floor. A dirty, soapy bucket was propped in the corner, the foam mop head sticking out of it missing chunks. The Boss lit a cigarette, shook his head. He dressed like a Green Beret: faux felt hat, military medals pinned to his lapels. Yellow, waxy fingers flicked ash near my boot.

"Have you heard of them maybe?" I asked.

The Boss narrowed his gaze, and I knew in that instant, as we squared off in the converted warehouse, that he would protect his own.

I recruited Bastardo and Kreeper, president of the Wicked Saints, telling them, "We're going hunting." We hit the bars in Polish Downtown and Polish Village, like Alex and his Droogs embarking on "a bit of the old ultraviolence."*

I didn't expect answers. But I still had to try. I began simply, approaching each bar and restaurant owner, posing the question the way a detective might initiate a murder investigation, except that I had no mug shots, no suspects, and no cooperative witnesses.

"Have you seen or heard of the Road Runners?" I got a lot of blank stares, frowns, and cupped ears, as if my voice were the problem. I tried sign language. Bastardo even flapped his arms. Eventually, we just resorted to punching.

---

* *A Clockwork Orange*, Anthony Burgess

I lost track after I slammed the seventh bartender's head into the counter. My rings were smeared with blood. Sweat stung my eyes. Bastardo swung a patron in circles, holding him by an arm and leg until the two blurred like a spinning teacup carnival ride. Bodies hit the floor. Strobe lights cast the scene in flashing black and white. Kreeper reminded me of a giant picking off small birds: "Take your shot, take your shot now before I eat you."

After a while I couldn't even feel my lower half. I stumbled over stools, sliced my hand on broken shot glasses, slipped in alcohol, tugged at random people's ears, and yelled, "If you see the Road Runners, tell them Big Pete is looking for them."

We moved like wrecking balls through bar after bar, leaving crushed ribs, broken teeth, clumps of hair on the wall. Bits of Polish flew at us; some patrons stuttered while others hid under tabletops, shielding their eyes from raining glass. Soon, we stopped even asking the question. What was the point? No one spoke English.

"We should split up."

The next night I tried a different approach.

"Road Runners?" I smiled at the pretty waitress.

She lit up. "Harley-Davidson?"

"Yeah okay, Harley-Davidson." I had downed at least three vodkas before she climbed on the back of my bike. As I maneuvered back alleys and deserted streets, repeating "Road Runners" and pointing to abandoned buildings, she giggled. *This was going nowhere.* As gorgeous as she was, I only wanted her for one thing: information. I pulled over.

She climbed off. "Harley-Davidson?"

I flashed my ring at her. "Married."

She started to strip.

"No, no." I dismounted, catching my foot on the brake and dragging the whole bike down. I landed in a mud puddle. *Fuck, fuck, fuck.*

"Harley-Davidson?"

"No Harley-Davidson tonight." I snapped my fingers and pointed to the bike. "Get back on this thing."

"I found a Road Runner," Kreeper told me the next day, grinning. We were at a fashion show. As a stripper writhed behind him, he spilled the details. He'd fled Stanis' bar just as the ambulance arrived. Several drunks had stumbled out, one with a broken jaw, the other with a small "nick" on his left arm.

"You *stabbed* him?"

"No, no, no, it was just a scratch," Kreeper continued. While some patrons left on stretchers, a lone biker pulled back, watched from the shadows. Kreeper had followed him as he weaved in and out of traffic and slowed at the light.

"Just the one?" I asked.

"So far."

"Where did he go?"

"Legacy's warehouse. The Road Runners rent the building next door."

"You knew about this, didn't you?" I said when I confronted Green Beret at his clubhouse/warehouse. It smelled like wet cardboard. The Legacy Boss feigned surprise.

"I take care of this."

"If you don't, I will."

He shut the door in my face.

The following week I called Green Beret for an update.

"Have you solved the problem?"

"I burned down their clubhouse," he said, his English suddenly fine.

I cradled the phone to my ear. What did he take me for, a fool? "That must have been pretty incredible, considering the building is cinder block."

"Bic."

"As in lighter?"

"Bic." He cleared his throat.

Now I knew the fucker was lying.

"Did you lose your thumb in the process?"

"What?"

"Bics don't stay lit unless you keep your thumb on the button."

Silence.

"We need to take them out," I said at the emergency meeting I'd called in the chiropractor's office. I'd drawn the vinyl blinds to shut out the street, and the room was nearly dark. The cushions squeaked under Bastardo's weight. He stared at the fish in the acquarium.

Kreeper picked at his club sandwich, removing the lettuce, tomato, and onions from the bacon. He folded the vegetables into his napkin.

"What the fuck's wrong with you two?" I threw up my hands.

Kreeper slurped his fountain drink. "We can't."

"Why not?"

"They're supporting the Hells Angels."

PART
II

21

SHELTER FROM THE STORM

Warm wind smacked my face, blew back my thick goatee, cut through my black jeans, combat boots, snub-nosed .38, and black vest. The roar of Harleys behind me shook the hand-painted signs along the road advertising fresh corn, apples, and tomatoes for sale at wooden stands. Around us were clumps of earth, rolling green hills, herds of bison, and a shock of blank sky near the Custer State Park in South Dakota's Black Hills, seventy miles from the annual Sturgis Motorcycle Rally, the largest gathering of bikers in the world.

Spread out in various packs and all scheduled to arrive by dim evening to our campsite, we rode several hundred miles a day out of Chicago's mean streets into a kind of blinding and unfamiliar calm.

Bob Dylan's lyrics crooned in my head—"in a world of steel-eyed death, and men who are fighting to be warm." I imagined the safe place he described and the siren in his song, who seduced creatures (like me) and gave them "shelter from the storm."

•   •   •

Rangers and local police found the broken-down white Ford pickup truck abandoned on an old logging road near Legion Lake Resort in Custer National Park. Inside were the remnants of a violent battle: blood spatter, spent bullet shells, an empty .40-caliber magazine, boxes of ammunition, hand grenades, Smith & Wesson pistols, high-powered rifles, a Häagen-Dazs ice cream wrapper, and a Hells Angels' T-shirt.

The shooter* later insisted The Outlaws ambushed him.† "I was terrified. I wasn't afraid. There was nine of them and two of us."

"But you would agree," the prosecutor reminded him, "that neither you, your partner,‡ nor your truck was hit with gunfire?"

The Hells Angels' lawyer answered for him, insisting it was "human nature" for his client to empty a gun into another human being.

"No one's getting near Sturgis." South Dakota state troopers and several federal marshals pulled over our pack. Their radios chattered crazily about the bloodshed of a sleepy resort town caused by an army of rival motorcycle thugs.

---

* Chad Wilson, a Canadian and member of the Dago chapter of the Hells Angels in San Diego
† Jurors acquitted them of attempted first-degree murder.
‡ John Midmore, a citizen of both Canada and Australia and a prospect of the Haney chapter of the Hells Angels in British Columbia, Canada

Suddenly *we* were the good guys, meriting a police escort into our makeshift campsite, situated in a primitive canyon bottom surrounded by woods (perfect for Hells Angels snipers). The rocky ground was littered with sharp twigs and blackened branches from the latest lightning storm. We had no phone service, no shelter, no port-o-potties, and only five showers.

"That's terrific—we're target practice."

Santa, the person responsible for the reservation, said, "Maybe we should call someone?"

I handed him my Nextel phone and suggested sarcastically that he dial 911.

"This is what happens when no one scouts the place first," I said directly into the phone's lens cap. *Intel, intel, intel.*

And while police combed the wooded hills with shotguns, searching for rogue bands of Hells Angels, Mr. Happy unloaded my golf cart from one of the chase vehicles and off I buzzed to the caretaker's cabin to pay the camping fees. I was, after all, the regional treasurer and the man in charge of the money.

Dick grinned as he took my final deposit—$101,000 for five days, not including "extras" like beer, Crown Royal, and Jack Daniel's (or picnic tables he offered to build us for $75 apiece) or the "anticipated damages" contract Santa willingly signed in advance. Dick's banter blasted noise in my head. We were sitting at his plastic drop-down table inside his kitchen. Crusted plates of mac and cheese littered the stove. A stuck bee buzzed on the screen, my monstrous shadow looming behind him as the sun set. As Dick prattled on, I focused on his mouth, the whoosh of air blowing in and out like an animal's pant.

He had already talked too long. Five minutes was my maximum for people unless they had some utility. It seemed somehow fitting that he kept a pen of six mangy wolves roped to a ponderosa pine near the entrance.

"Bring me a pistol," I said, and off Mr. Happy trotted. He knew the score—*Just don't kill anyone* (unless they're Hells Angels). I never traveled without heat. I stashed an arsenal in our mobile home—a MAC 10, .357 Magnum, .40-caliber Glock, and hunting knives—and for a fleeting moment calm replaced the flashes of General George Custer* that replayed in my head.

But the sensation was short–lived, as Mr. Happy slapped a derringer in the palm of my hand and reported, "The cops found several Hells Angels' outposts in the woods."

As darkness fell, real pandemonium set in. Outlaws positioned their RVs and trailers along the perimeter of the bowl, forming a wall against potential snipers. Our police escort rode into the hills, their taillights slashing across the handlebars of the many Harleys parked on the edge of the pit.

Outlaws slumped against pines, slept in tents on patches of dirt, sucked cigarettes, huddled around an unlit fire pit,

---

* At "Custer's Last Stand," a force of seven hundred men led by Custer suffered a severe defeat. Five of the 7th Calvary's twelve companies were annihilated; Custer was killed. Custer's actions and the battle have been studied extensively by historians.

and swallowed can after can of Miller Lite in what eerily resembled a ready-made grave. I watched as our leader, Joker, disappeared into the woods to stay in his girlfriend's condo, leaving his loyal minions poised for an ambush. "What do you expect?" I groused to Mr. Happy. "He's a trucker. What else can he do but piss and drive?"

By day two Joker's name ended most sentences like punctuation.

We remained captive in a wooded prison, mostly drunk and stumbling over logs and discarded beer cans. Some members had already depleted the private stash of Jack Daniel's they had brought with them in their saddlebags.

Cigarette butts littered the ground. We played no music, had no women to distract us, and if we did speak our voices echoed. Bodies formed silhouettes in the shadows. The stench of urine filled the night air from the rows of port-o-potties lining the perimeter. Every branch snap sounded like gunfire.

Ho Jo drew a circle in the dirt with his cane.

"Hey, Pete, what's the plan?" He had been up all night with Butch, who was groggy from weed and booze.

The *plan,* I wanted to tell him, was simple: Stay alive.

Clusters of Outlaws stood in various parts of the campsite holding their cell phones in midair, hoping for a brief connection to the outside.

"Hey." Jaws ushered me over. He'd managed to get a signal. "Want to call Bun?"

The mere mention of Debbie's name calmed me. The news no doubt had broadcast an all-out biker war. She probably hadn't slept. We had an understanding that, no matter what, I always checked in with her, always let her know I was safe. I snatched Jaws's phone and dialed Debbie's number. One ring, two, the phone crackled, three, *please pick up,* four, "Hello?" She sounded so far away.

"Don't worry, Bun, I'm okay."

Click. The line went dead.

By day three we had all tired of waiting to be silenced by high-powered rifles designed to drop us before we even heard a bang. Joker and Santa convinced the police to let us ride into Deadwood, the town that made Wild Bill Hickok infamous.

We rode en masse, with our police escort looking like a human zoo on wheels. We dressed in full colors, grease-caked jeans, sleeveless black vests with top and bottom rockers, goggles, capes, bandannas, swastika tattoos, and twin lightning bolts, the letters OFFO* and FTW† inked on our arms just below the diamond one-percenter patch. We raced down the highway, some of us still drunk from the night before, traveling in unison at one speed—fast.

We never made it into Deadwood. "This is far enough," a state trooper said, then guided us into a parking lot half a mile from town and informed us we "had four hours to explore."

"Fuck this," I said, and passed the time with Mr. Happy

---

* Outlaws Forever Forever Outlaws
† Fuck the World

playing slots in a nearby pizza joint. We ordered slice after slice of soggy bread spread with tomato paste surrounded by a bar slick with grease and plastic checkered tablecloths. A young waitress with fluffy cheeks and wide hips skittered in and out of the kitchen; her wild-eyed stare reminded me of a psychotic rabbit's.

At dusk, we mounted our bikes again and thundered out of the parking lot, gunning our engines, all of us acutely aware we were in hostile territory bordered by woods and shadows and stretches of highway that disappeared over hills and curves.

Bob Dylan's "Shelter from the Storm" beat in my head: "suddenly . . . she was standin' there"—the mule deer. The animal came from out of nowhere, leaving me no time to brake or swerve. If I did I might be killed or mowed down as the hundreds of bikes behind me crashed, skidded into trees, decapitated limbs, crushed heads, splintered bones, and pierced muscle and flesh.

I didn't fear death; I feared a *stupid* death. And I certainly wasn't going to be the *cause* of multiple fatalities involving my own men. A headline flashed in my mind's eye: *Boss and Regional Treasurer of The Chicago Outlaws Motorcyle Gang, Third-Largest City in U.S., Dead from a Deer.*

I accelerated, aiming to split the fucking thing in half. Suddenly I was in the mood to destroy something beautiful. I slammed into the animal at forty-five miles an hour. Blood spattered my front tire. Small specks hit my face. The deer soared into a roadside ditch. The impact jolted my bike and sent sharp pain through my arms, but I held on as bike after bike roared past me on the highway.

Some Outlaws gave me the thumbs-up signal; others whooped and peeled their tires. Only Bull, a brother from the Springfield chapter, stopped as I pulled over to the side of the road with a busted brake.

"You need help?"

Wind blew through the pines. A prickly sensation hit the back of my neck just above my blue eye tattoo, the second of thirty-eight I had inked on my body in the last year.

A Fed rolled down his window. "Hey, big man, are you okay?"

"*I'm* fine. How's the deer?"

"Dead. How did you *do* that? You didn't even tip your bike?"

"Simple physics."

He stared at me for a few seconds as if waiting for further explanation. And then off he went, stranding me on the side of the road dressed in my Outlaw vest with a deer carcass stinking up the space around me.

"Why don't you head back to camp," I said to Bull. I wasn't being a martyr; *I just didn't want to be responsible for another person's life.* He nodded and sped off, looking all too eager to leave. I put my bike in neutral and rolled down the hill, through the next stop sign, and past a row of South Dakota state troopers.

"Hey," one yelled. Though the moon shined in the night sky, he still wore his mirrored sunglasses.

"Brake's busted," I said. "I just hit a fucking deer."

"Did you report it?"

"I think I just did."

"It's a criminal offense in these parts to strike an animal and leave it rotting in a ditch without reporting the kill." The trooper stared at me, hands on his hips, tall, skinny, looking every bit like a kid who'd spent his youth stuffed inside a locker.

I couldn't believe it—all this for a fucking deer? I caught my reflection in his glasses; I could have swallowed him whole, gun belt and all.

"Do you have a permit?" another trooper interrupted my thoughts.

"For what?"

"Weapons."

"Sure," I lied.

"Empty your pockets."

I smothered a smile: My snub-nosed .38 was safely tucked inside a hidden liner in my vest.

"I'm going to run you."

I felt like I had been dropped into some weird cartoon. *Run* me? I knew he wouldn't find anything. I waited silently for him to go through the motions.

"He checks out." The trooper looked disappointed. "No warrants. You're free to go."

"I want protection."

"You want—"

"I'm from Chicago," I cut him off. "I'm lost in these woods. I'm being hunted. You're the cops. Protect me."

I could tell I had really stumped them.

"You want an escort back to your campsite?" Skinny Locker Kid said, stumbling over his words. By now he had removed his sunglasses.

"Yes," I said. "You wouldn't want to be an accessory to murder, would you?"

The cops took me as far as Custer National Park and sped off. As I rolled into camp with my broken bike, throbbing wrists, and blood-spattered beard, Joker trotted up and demanded cash; they needed "limes for the Bloody Marys."

"Someone needs to go grocery shopping," he said.

Dick, the caretaker, stood on his porch, hands in his pockets, perfectly deformed, like a wooded night creature. He grinned as I approached, as if the very smell of me made him salivate money.

"Jack Daniel's for everyone," I said. If this was going to be it, we were going to go down in style.

"You want a tab?" Dick chuckled.

"Yeah, open bar."

Day four was a blur. Most of the Outlaws slept (hungover from the night before), smoked, and started inane conversations about rule interpretations. I really disliked camping. The thought of sleeping on twigs and rocks on a tent floor had about as much appeal to me as swatting flies at a hot summer picnic. I had had enough. Some brothers from the Florida chapter decided to shoot footage for a documentary they were making—*The Outlaws at Sturgis*. The event, after all, was a big deal, they stressed: two years in the making, requiring lots of planning. Joker and Santa spent hours reviewing with "the Commission" options and logistics and food. Without a National Boss, Joker and Santa had to convince five hundred members to ride (no small feat, since most didn't even *like* motorcycles) across the country for five days to attend a venue where they weren't even welcome. In the end, Milwaukee Jack destroyed the footage, fearful the film actually made the Outlaws look *bad* and not just bad*ass*.

PS: This was after he announced on day five that *he* was running for office. PPS: He thought he was well qualified (he was a trucker). PPPS: During his reign he befriended Charles Falco,* the only informant to ever successfully bring down a patched member on RICO charges.

"Let's get the fuck out of here," I said. I helped Mr. Happy load the bikes onto trailers and cover them with tarps, then climbed into my mobile home with Ho Jo and Animal (a member of Ho Jo's chapter) and let Mr. Happy navigate the narrow roads home.

"Hey, Pete," Ho Jo asked after a while.

"What's up?"

"You think we could stop somewhere for food?"

I glanced out my window. State troopers had pulled over a cluster of Outlaws, no doubt because their bikes still broadcast the club's insignia.

---

* See *Vagos, Mongols, and Outlaws: My Infiltration of America's Deadliest Biker Gangs*, by Kerrie Droban and Charles Falco.

"Yeah, sure." Mr. Happy pulled into the next gas station.

"Hey, Pete." Ho Jo was grinning. "What kind of cookies do you like?"

Cookies?

"Surprise me."

Ho Jo returned carrying grocery bags full of cookies.

He climbed in, pulled out his favorite, Windmills, and offered me one.

"I couldn't decide," he said. Crumbs spotted his T-shirt. "I bought every brand they had. 'Heaven Scent' looked pretty cool."

And that was the last image I had of Ho Jo before he was murdered.

22

HO JO

Newspapers reported his senseless death as if he were some nameless Outlaw "gunned down as he locked up his tattoo shop." Journalists glossed over the detail about Ho Jo's bodyguard, who followed behind him into the street and somehow "narrowly missed the gunshots."

In the last year I had been to nineteen funerals; odds were pretty good that *someone* was going to die on the way home from a National, or a funeral—fifty-fifty chance. Ho Jo's funeral, a massive tribute that drew Outlaws from several regions, was held on a blustery February morning in the Red Region several miles from the Waterbury clubhouse in Connecticut and nearly eleven hundred miles from Chicago. My whole chapter attended, along with the Black Pistons. I had given each a button with Ho Jo's face on it to wear on their vests.

At a chilly thirty-five degrees, I rode as a passenger in Bastardo's truck. And, since closed spaces made me claustrophobic, I dressed light, in a sleeveless T-shirt and hoodie, and left behind my leather trench.

Before leaving for the funeral home, Jake, the Regional Boss of the Red Region, rapped his knuckles on my window.

I opened it a crack.

"Ho Jo would have wanted you to ride his bike and lead the procession." His breath blew white.

Wind cut into my cheeks like glass. *Ho Jo and I had always been close, but never could I have anticipated he would relinquish his bike; Outlaws were sometimes buried with their motorcycles, the cremated remains stored in a Harley gas tank, spread over a favorite stretch of road, or dumped at a bike rally. Ho Jo had just bestowed the highest honor on me, and all I could think about was finding a coat.*

"Sounds great," I said.

Bastardo peeled off his gloves and slapped them in my hands as I stepped into the frigid temperatures.

Motherfucker. I straddled Ho Jo's Harley Softail Fat Boy and shoved the key into the ignition. *Come on, Ho Jo, you've always come through for me. Don't fail me now.* Hundreds of Outlaws idled behind me, anxiously waiting for the bike to respond to the accelerator like a bucking horse to a whip and scorch the pavement with a fiery blast from the chrome tailpipes.

My teeth chattered; my hoodie blew like a thin layer of skin. It was easily a twenty-mile ride from the clubhouse to the funeral home and another *twenty-five* miles to the cemetery. *Motherfucker.* I shoved the key in the ignition. *Click.*

Santa roared up, his bandanna covering his mouth just below his eyes. "What's the matter?"

"She won't start."

"Can we jump her?" Santa waved over Bastardo.

"Make sure you turn that fucker off first."

Santa looked confused.

"If the car engine is *on* it will ruin the bike's regulator." Members of Ho Jo's chapter hooked cables from the car to the bike's battery. *Come on, Ho Jo.* The light flashed on. Nothing.

They fiddled with the cables a few minutes more, trying different angles, stepping back, hands on hips, caucusing the problem before I finally interjected, "Time's up. We need to get to the funeral home so we can lead the hearse to the cemetery."

Santa mounted his bike. "You know where you're going?"

"Yeah, sure," I lied. At this point all I cared about was defrosting.

I folded like a lawn chair into Bastardo's truck. "You know where you're going?"

He grinned at me and followed Animal's pack, the noise deafening, like bombers passing overhead. The Outlaws commandeered the freeway like Genghis Khan, Morgan's Raiders, and *The Wild One* all at once. Several miles later, Animal pulled into a gas station; *he* was following closely behind *another* pack.

"What's going on?" I buzzed down the window, and a blast of cold air smacked my face.

"One of the brothers ran out of gas." Animal watched as the member "topped off." Soon the whole pack had lined up and one by one filled up.

"What the fuck is wrong with all of you?" My mind raced with sniper scenarios. After all, we were trespassing through Hells Angels territory. *Who the fuck gets gas on the way to a funeral?*

"Get back on your bike," I barked to Animal. "Let's move."

None of us knew where we were going. We followed Animal, who followed another pack who led us in circles, zooming four abreast through the curves, exceeding the speed limit, until finally we arrived at the funeral home, cresting the hill like a large mass . . . too late. We parked six blocks away in the only available spaces. I hobbled the distance, shivering, wind beating against me, just in time to watch the processional of Outlaws exit the service.

Later, at the cemetery, I pulled Ho Jo's Boss, Lumpy, aside and told him the gas story. He nodded, his wind-burned cheeks turned a brighter shade of red, and within minutes he'd dispatched enforcers to "handle Gas Man." And while Ho Jo's casket was being lowered into the ground, chapter soldiers dragged Gas Man behind a stone slab and pummeled both his eyes. When the Outlaw emerged minutes later to rejoin the service, he looked bruised and bloody.

Hundreds of bikes rolled by two at a time in procession to pay their respects, sounding like dirty thunder washing over tombstones. Arms initiated the rifle volley, the twenty-one-gun salute reserved for veterans. A bugler played Taps. Jack presented me with one of the discharged shells and returned Ho Jo's gold medallion, the one I had given to him as a Christmas gift.

He was buried in his vest, and although he was a member of the Red Region, he had embroidered on his bottom rocker, *"Chicago North Side Crew."*

"He was at my clubhouse so often I actually gave him keys," I said to Lumpy.

Later, in the quiet of my hotel room, I honored Ho Jo too. I placed his buttoned face on the tiny desk reserved for businessmen and cut a perfect line of cocaine across his smiling eyes.

The financial fallout from Sturgis continued with Dick's final bill.

"What the fuck is this? Twelve thousand dollars for cigarette butts, seventy-five dollars apiece for picnic tables?"

"It's pretty busy in the garage today." Santa wheezed. "I'm putting in a transmission." *I had lost count of the number of transmissions Santa had repaired.*

"Why am I still talking?"

"We signed a contract."

No, you *signed a contract, you fuck.*

"We're paying for littering now?" I felt my blood pressure rise.

"Can we meet about this?"—Santa's solution to conflict.

"I don't want to meet," one of the Bosses complained. "He just rambles for hours and hours about nothing."

"Have an agenda," I warned Santa. "No one has time to sit around for six or seven hours."

The following week, thirteen chapter Bosses crowded in my office and complained about Sturgis. Santa scribbled pages and pages of notes about his own ineptitude.

After a couple of hours, I grabbed a sandwich from the cooler.

More scribbling, and then Santa's apology: "At least the food was good."

23

THE COSMIC RIDERS

Apology was not enough. The Sturgis debacle reinforced for me the perils of being *part* of an organization and not in *charge* of the organization. And while I considered plans to recoup my own financial losses, opportunity came quite unexpectedly, almost like a sign from the cosmos (*I believed in that shit*). I awoke one morning from a rare nap and answered a call on my house phone from an unknown number (something I never did on principle). The heavily accented voice on the other end immediately got my attention: "I understand you're the chairman of the COC?"

I sat bolt upright in bed and felt the blood drain from my body. "How did you get this number?" My heart raced.

"I found it off the Web site—off the COC page?"

I relaxed a little. "What do you want?"

"I'm with the American Cruisers in Southern Illinois."

"What do you want?" I repeated.

"Is it okay for us to fly our colors here?"

"Who told you that you *could*?"

"Sonny."

"Sonny?"

"Yeah."

"As in Sonny *Barger*?"

"Yeah."

I was now wide awake. I threw the covers off and looked at the caller ID again. "You actually *spoke* to him?"

"Well, not exactly," the caller faltered.

"You *do* realize Illinois is not an Angel state." I cradled the phone to my ear. "Sonny has nothing to do with what goes on in Chicago."

Silence.

"What's your name?"

"Brad."

"I've never heard of you."

"My wife and I saw this stuff on the Internet." The caller's voice faded like background noise. *Wife?*

"I'm going to call you back, *Brad*."

I hung up the phone and sat in the dark for what seemed like several minutes. A plan formed in my head: What if *Brad* and his old lady joined an all-inclusive motorcycle club, one that accepted everyone—broads, shines, Chinks, gays, couples, single riders?

"Completely nondiscriminatory," I pointed out as I explained my plan to Mr. Happy.

"You want to create a fake motorcycle club?"

"That's right."

"Why?"

"Money." I was already planning to keep this venture a

secret from the Outlaws. But I trusted Mr. Happy, and I needed his help if I was going to pull off the ruse. "Think about the earning potential. We could charge every prospective member a fee to join: two hundred dollars if they want to start their own chapter, a hundred twenty if they join as a couple, seventy-five to buy their patch. Then we could charge for business cards, T-shirts, and other merchandise. How many members belong to the American Cruisers?"

"I don't know, maybe a thousand?"

My head spun with possibilities.

"We would only need a couple of guys to make the fake club look legitimate."

"Posers?"

"Black Pistons." The rush off the planning was better than a line of coke. "We could recruit this *Brad* and his broad out of Southern Illinois to form the second chapter of the fake club. It'll be great."

I called Brad the next morning. "I know a little club here that you may want to consider."

"Really?" There was static on the line. "Send me the information and I'll review it with my wife."

I twisted the phone cord around my thumb. *Well, shit, I wasn't expecting* that *response.*

"Sure, fine. I'll send over the stuff in a couple of days."

Had I completely lost my mind?

"I'll be taking a little trip," I informed my Outlaw chapter later that afternoon, and over the next four days I worked feverishly, forgoing sleep, food, even showers to create the fictitious Cosmic Riders.

"You're killing yourself," Mr. Happy said.

"I'm having a blast."

I designed two one-piece patches for "The Cosmic Riders Association"—"His and Hers" sets. Male members could order from the computer a wolf howling at the moon; females, a white-winged Pegasus. I made the Cosmic Riders an "association" rather than an "MC" so that real one-percenters would pay no attention to them. After all, *my whole objective was to make money, not get anyone killed.*

I created a Web site, wrote a mission statement, invented bylaws and a constitution, and even crafted an e-mail address. In the span of three days, I posted hundreds of messages to the site, pretending to be different bikers commenting on past events. I even wrote messages about upcoming runs and charitable fund-raisers, hoping to entice prospective members into believing the Cosmic Riders were thriving.

The ruse reminded me of the time I owned and operated a small cable company in the city and decided to create competition by forming three additional companies (all mine) and encouraging contractors to bid against each other. None suspected they were speaking to *me* at all three companies.

I read the mission statement aloud:

"We are a family-based motorcycle club comprised of men and women. All riders are welcome . . ."

I paused and added, ". . . on *all* types of bikes: sport, mini, Schwinn. . . ."

I had fun with it, borrowing from my college writing days. "The mission of the Cosmic Riders," I punched into the computer, "is the bonding of our membership into a brotherhood and sisterhood, sharing the exhilaration of the open road." *Maybe "exhilaration" was too big a word?* I left it alone. "We also intend our national organization to be the central chapter for our members at large for the exchange of experiences. . . ." *How else was I going to maintain control?*

"The primary goal is for all participants to have a good time. If it isn't fun it isn't worth doing." This last line became the club's motto and ran as a banner on the bottom in bold italics.

After a few more reads, I considered adding the disclaimer that the Cosmic Riders, "though charitable," did not endorse any particular cause.

"Maybe you should explain the patches?" Debbie suggested.

Good idea.

I designed them based on a tarot card; the patch denoted "balance," and the club represented "a small part of the harmonious spiritual unfettered laws of the human spirit."

"Too much?"

Debbie just shook her head.

"They're a hundred-percent club," I explained to Junior, president of the Black Pistons. Why one-percenters insisted on hundreds of pages of useless bylaws no one ever read or followed puzzled me. Outlaws needed to keep things simple, *to* do whatever the fuck they wanted in twenty-four hours as long as they worked eight, slept eight, and partied eight.

• •   •

"What's in this for me?" Junior asked, considering my proposal. His father was an Outfit guy, head of the Cicero crew. Junior grew up in The Life, understood duality, secrecy, and urgency.

"Money."

"You want me to pose as a Black Piston and a Cosmic Rider and involve a few more Black Pistons to keep up the pretense?"

"They just have to model in the vests as Cosmic Riders."

"So this is a side deal? The Outlaws are not involved?"

"Right." I didn't see a reason to split proceeds.

"What would *I* have to do?"

"Be the Boss of the Cosmic Riders."

"This is just on paper, right?"

"Mostly," I said.

" 'Cause you know I can't ride a bike."

Operation Cosmic Riders went better than anticipated. Brad and his old lady signed up immediately, paid the dues, and bought the "His" and "Her" vests. They sent me pictures of the two of them at Busch Gardens, hand in hand, sporting their beer caps, beaming for the camera.

I called Junior for daily updates. "How's it going?"

"It's getting a little out of control," he complained. Chapters were cropping up all over the country. "The fake club now has substantial membership."

Three chapters had formed in Illinois, two in Kentucky, one in Indiana, and one in Michigan. I solicited Brad to be the national vice president in charge of recruiting and developed "Welcome Kits" complete with framed charter certificates that chapter heads could hang on their clubhouse wall.

Then one afternoon I received the dreaded call: "Brad's done," Junior said. "He plans to join a national motorcycle club."

24

THE BUSINESS OF BUSINESS

While Junior covered for me, I listened to complaints about Ray Rayner's chapter, how Elgin extorted support clubs into *paying* them to attend their parties.

"So," Santa scribbled, "you're saying if Elgin gives you fifteen tickets to sell for them and you only sell five, you're responsible for the balance of the unsold tickets?"

I marveled that Santa worked as a CPA and did taxes for Outlaws and citizens.

"Unacceptable." Santa put his pen down. "I'll handle this."

But as usual, nothing happened.

"You need to take care of the Elgin problem," Hobbs, head of Low Lyfz, complained to me the next month. "Ray Rayner is out of control."

I met Santa in his "office," a five-by-five-foot closet with no windows. Our shoulders touched. My heart raced, and I struggled to breathe. Santa lit a cigarette, and I worried that the ash would blow onto my chin.

"Ray Rayner's chapter is treating the support clubs like his personal slaves," I pointed out to him again. He regularly ordered club supporters to fix his roof, repair his shed, mix cement for his garage project, run silly errands at their own expense, and contribute to his chapter's endless (and frivolous) fund-raisers.

"Unacceptable." Santa puffed and stabbed his cigarette into the walls. "I'll take care of this."

But again, nothing happened.

"Pete, they're drinking for free," Beast from Unwanted complained to me privately. "We're losing money. They're keeping my guys up until seven A.M. They're going behind the bar."

That was the ultimate insult. The support clubs had no recourse for a bully dressed in an Outlaw vest.

Don't get me wrong, I could care less about preserving some twisted existence that confused right and wrong, or defended the Outlaws' predatory nature. I had my own agenda—I needed the clubs' support to control Chicago, particularly in the wake of the Outlaws' puppet "leadership."

Santa shook his head in disgust. "I'll have a talk with them. I'll have this problem solved in two weeks."

Again, nothing happened.

I had a better solution for Beast: "Next time Ray Rayner's chapter orders drinks, charge them. If Elgin refuses to pay, tell them the drinks are going on Big Pete's tab."

"What the fuck is up with Elgin?" a Regional Boss from the Florida chapter asked me the next week.

"You'll have to be more specific," I said.

"They're bringing their old ladies with them wherever they go."

It was true: Ray Rayner actually suggested skipping Church once in February because it interfered with Valentine's Day.

"It's embarrassing," I said to Santa.

"Unacceptable."

But some affronts required intervention. Once I noticed an old fucker hobble with a cane into an Outlaw party, dressed in a probate vest.

"Who is *that*?" I asked Ray Rayner.

"He's my probate."

"I know *what* he is—*why* is he?"

"What's that supposed to mean?"

"How *old* is he?"

"Fifty-two."

"Why are we accepting geriatrics into the club?"

"Big Dog did."

I vaguely remembered that call. "He's a good guy, Pete," Big Dog from Kankakee had pled his case.

"He's old."

"I like him."

"He's too old—no," I repeated.

"I'm calling Santa."

I pulled Santa aside at a party.

"Did you tell Big Dog he could accept an over-the-hill probate into his club?"

Santa's eyes widened. "I know nothing about that."

"He's the one who gave me permission," Big Dog said, indignant and insistent over the line.

"Unacceptable," I said to Santa. "Take care of it or I will."

But Santa didn't. Instead, he ordered Big Dog to take the fall and send the probate packing. The probate should have sat in a chair while a national enforcer drilled both eyes until they bruised and filled with pus.

"So, I can keep my probate right?" Ray Rayner said.

Why bother? Why not just *purchase* Chicago rockers and dispense with the whole probating shit? The Outlaws, after all, were just grown men playing army.

Indigo, the new vice president of the South Side, caught my arm and whispered in broken English, "I just spotted a few California rockers."

Alarm shot through me. *Angels here at the party?* "What's the *top* say?" I scanned the partygoers, but the crowd was too dense.

"Not sure." Indigo's head came up to my elbow.

"Go look and count," I said.

A few minutes passed, and Indigo trotted up to me, sweaty, anxious. "There's two of them. The rockers say 'Sons of Anarchy.'" He pronounced the last syllable as a "ch."

"What?"

Indigo repeated the name.

"That's a fucking television show!"

At the next Regional Bosses' chapter meeting, Santa produced the "Rules" he received at the last National Convention.

The list exceeded three pages. *Never mind that we were supposed to be the one percent of the population that broke ninety-nine percent of all rules.*

"I can't read these with a straight face," I said as I flipped through the pages. "Rule #20: DON'T WEAR 'SUPPORT' ON THE BACK OF A T-SHIRT? Rule #21: IF A BROTHER FROM ONE REGION EXCHANGES A T-SHIRT WITH A BROTHER FROM ANOTHER REGION THAT BROTHER CAN'T WEAR THAT SHIRT. Why?"

"If something goes down in a region that's not that brother's region and the T-shirt reads 'Chicago' on the bottom rocker, for example, then *the shirt* will bring heat to that other region."

I waited for Santa's lips to stop moving. "What?"

Santa opened his mouth again in protest, but I cut him off. "If something goes down in someone else's region, don't you think Feds will review surveillance cameras, physical descriptions, recordings? They're not going to rely on a fucking T-shirt as identification."

"It's a rule," Santa whimpered.

"How are you going to enforce this?"

"It's in the constitution," Santa said.

"Then it's time for a revision."

"We're supposed to follow the rules," Santa repeated. *I couldn't believe what I was hearing. This went against everything I believed in. It seemed there were more rules to being a good criminal than there were to being a good CPA.*

"We're one-percenters. We aren't *supposed* to do anything." I was tempted to design a square patch with an embroidered "100%" and hand it out at the next meeting, but instead I designed my own T-shirt, black on black, and in shiny *black* lettering printed, "Go Fuck Yourself."

As if the rules were not bad enough, there was the mysterious disappearance of the $55,000 brothers had contributed over the last two years toward funerals, regional dues, and Taco's defense fund.

"What happened to the money?" I asked Santa.

"Can I call you back? I'm putting in a transmission."

"I'm coming over."

Some conversations had to be done in person. I waded through the smoke in Santa's tiny office. It was the size of two airplane bathrooms shoved together; no room to pace. I stood, pressed against the wall, inhaling smoke and feeling light-headed.

"What happened to the fifty-five thousand dollars?"

Santa looked at me, his eyes bugging.

"Fucking Bull." He took a long puff on his cigarette. And it occurred to me that "Fucking Joker" had now morphed into "Fucking Bull," Santa's appointed treasurer.

"A lot of chapters just simply aren't paying," Santa said.

"Why?"

"I know nothing about that"—his standard line. "You'd have to ask Bull."

"I plan on it." I organized a meeting with the chapter treasurers to find out how $55,000 just disappeared.

Two weeks later the treasurers gathered in my office. Some brought receipts, cash, or handwritten ledgers, and I went around the table firing off questions; it was a little like playing Russian roulette, only I never got to pull the trigger.

"Turns out," I reported to Santa, "the most any of the chapters owe totals a hundred bucks."

Santa blanched.

"Taco's lawyer still needs to be paid," I said. "And the Outlaw Nation is owed a percentage."

"Fucking Bull," Santa mumbled.

"Fucking Bull" was recovering from a bike wreck. He hobbled into my office looking like smashed meat. The side of his head was shaved and stiches zippered across his scalp. He propped his crutches on the wall and eased into a chair.

"What happened to fifty-five thousand dollars?"

"My head is going to explode." Bull massaged his temple. "I'm so doped up right now I can't even think."

"He's out," I told Santa. Either Bull really stole the money and Santa was truly oblivious, or Santa had conspired with Bull. It didn't matter; I couldn't prove anything.

But I *could* do damage control. And so I assigned my trusted friend and brother Maurice to oversee the operations and gave Santa a debit card. This way I could track his expenses even when he lied.

Debits reflected dinners at Cracker Barrel, Dairy Queen, hotel expenses for parties he attended "in town" and stayed over for two nights.

"The fucker lives a hundred thirty miles from Chicago," Maurice remarked.

"So?"

"So he drives up the night before, stays for two hours,

and leaves the next day. That's a 'write-off' for him." Maurice chuckled. "Wouldn't it just be easier to kick him out?"

Truth? I didn't want Santa's job. I wanted to control him. And though he was technically my superior, he deferred to me. I had him exactly where I wanted him: powerless. And it was important he understood that.

25

HIGH NOON

Rockford, Illinois, a town I would ordinarily only stop to take a piss in while traveling between Chicago and Madison, was home to a struggling Outlaw chapter with, at most, six members. When they threw a party, twelve people on average attended.

"Let's show them some love," I announced at the next COC meeting, and rallied hundreds of bikers from thirty-seven chapters for the run. Rockford was within my "sphere of influence"; 25 percent of the clubs in the COC, after all, were located north of Chicago.

But no one had a clue where the new Rockford clubhouse had moved. So the pack of two hundred bikers agreed to convene at the Belvidere Oasis, a rest area off the freeway, to get directions from Tank, the lone scout Outlaw from the Rockford chapter.

The image reflected in my rearview mirror of hundreds of bikes undulating over rolling hills was very nearly orgasmic. The bike united us, made us all "outlaws," no matter our club. We became a *force,* defying rules, limits, patterns; splitting lines; disrupting traffic. Without the bike, we were just men in costume, gathering nightly in bars to drink, fight, and score. The bike set us apart; it defined us, gave us purpose.

Debbie once marveled at my transformation from Just Pete to Big Pete to Biker Pete. My "whole face changed," she said, when I straddled my Harley; I "radiated confidence" and "exuded a nearly superhuman strength"—man and his machine—mirrored by the riders rumbling behind me. We were so much more, she went on, than a "cult of thugs."

Tank roared into the Oasis. "Got to keep our eyes out."

"Why's that?" I tipped my head, peered at him over my sunglasses.

"Angels."

I knew they had a clubhouse in Rockford. Their big supporter, the Hell's Henchmen, had staked the territory since before the 1994 bombings.

"They're having a party," Tank said.

"How far is their clubhouse from yours?"

"Just down the street."

"Let's go then." I revved my engine.

"Are you sure that's a good idea?"

"Lead the way."

Tank hesitated, then said, "Okay—we just have to keep our eyes out."

I didn't bother correcting him. Instead I signaled to the hundreds of bikers lined up behind me. "Follow me."

We roared out of the Oasis, two abreast, tight formation, like a motorized army. A lone cop was parked on the side of the road; he stumbled out of his patrol car, dropped his radio, watched his hat blow off in a gust of wind.

I stopped at the next red light. The bikes fell into line.

"The Hells Angels' house is right there." Tank pointed down the street to a nondescript structure with tinfoil on the windows, bags of garbage on the lawn, bikes parked askew in the driveway.

I gave the signal to charge.

"Wait, wait, what are you doing?" Tank slid his glasses onto his forehead. Large lobotomy eyes stared at me.

"I'm going."

"Hey, Boss," Cockroach said as he pulled away from the pack. "I don't think that's such a good idea."

"Did I ask you?"

"They're HAs." Cockroach sat ramrod straight on his bike, his greasy whiskers twitching. Knuckle gloves covered his dirty fingernails. "We need to keep our eyes out."

"The next person who says that is going to wear a probate vest." I jumped the starter and roared through the light; all two hundred bikes followed.

"I don't know about this, Boss." Tank's worry blew into the wind.

I waved to several stray Hells Angels on the porch. *Shit,* they yelled, and leapt from their lawn chairs, darted inside, bolted shut the dilapidated front door.

I lit a cigarette.

Loud thuds resounded from the garage. Panties and heels littered the walkway, and I heard a few broads scream. A Hells Angel skittered across the lawn and raced to padlock the chain-link fence. A few more hauled bike parts inside. One tripped, cut his knee on a broken bottle. Burning embers from a makeshift fire pit blew into the sky.

I took a puff.

Someone tore a corner of tinfoil from the top window and shoved an assault rifle through the crack.

"Fuck, did you see that?"

Truth: I had no idea as to my next move. If Hells Angels fired at us, I fully intended to return the bullets. I inhaled slowly. The line of bikes idled in ready position. I dropped my cigarette into the dirt and stomped out the butt.

I slid my hand inside my vest, rested my finger on the trigger of my .38, all eyes on me, waiting for my signal. Seconds ticked into minutes.

Nothing. The rifle in the window stayed pointed directly at me. The clubhouse was suddenly eerily quiet except for the roar of our motorcycles. I imagined most inside were either passed out or drunk.

"Now what?" Tank whispered.

"We party."

The bike pack coasted slowly down the street, keeping tight formation, until it reached the Rockford clubhouse. Rows and rows of bikes parked along the street and curb, some dangerously close to the Hells Angels' block, and when our various members funneled passed the six Rockford Outlaws, they had a little swagger.

Santa slurped a bowl of wedding soup; clear, thin liquid dribbled down his beard. Mongol, Boss of the Invaders MC, headquartered in Cedar Lake, had insisted we meet to discuss the continued viability of the peace treaty established between clubs. Chicago was off limits to the Invaders without the Outlaws' blessing, and the Outlaws could not enter St. Louis without first notifying the Invaders.

"I heard what happened last week." Mongol studied the menu.

"What's he talking about?" Santa's spoon paused midair.

"Some big guy with black hair and a black goatee challenged Hells Angels in Rockford."

"You know anything about this?" Santa asked as he continued to slurp.

"No idea." I swirled a piece of bread into a plate of oil.

"He ruined their party. They're pissed. Lost revenue. They're blaming the Outlaws."

"Wow." I took a bite of bread. "I wonder who *that* was?"

Santa glared at me. Mongol excused himself to use the bathroom. "What the fuck was that all about?"

"I have no idea."

"Hands off—you know my policy on the Hells Angels." Santa raised his hands in the air. "Hands off."

"No hands were *on*. All I did was park across the street and smoke a cigarette."

Santa rolled his eyes.

"Elgin is dropping out of the COC," Ray Rayner announced the next week. "It's not personal; it's politics. It's just not working for us anymore. Besides, you're COC guy," he said, expressing the term with his fingers. "We're *Outlaws*. It's confusing."

"He started his own COC," Kreeper said. "He's selling tickets to his welcome party and promises decent food."

"Are you worried?" Debbie asked me later.

" 'Worry' is not part of my vocabulary. No one will buy tickets to his stupid event. There's one thing Bozo and his circus clowns will never have."

"What's that?"

"Me."

Ray Rayner missed the goal of the COC: unification, an MC world with no rivals. The Chicago Outlaws had belonged to the NCOM coalition for six years once, and unfortunately, they still thought the organization was all about domination.

"What you all need to realize," I addressed attendees at the next patch-holders' meeting in Oklahoma City, "is that the man makes the patch, the patch doesn't make the man."

The convention was held in a resort, and later I relaxed with Debbie on the patio area of the hotel bar, overlooking a grassy lawn dotted with delicate white umbrellas, pretty wooden folding chairs, and draped roses. Wedding scenery.

"Nice speech," a Phantom Lord said as he pulled up a chair.

"Name's TK." He handed me his business card. "Support Your Local 81" was flashed across his vest. Lanky, with a tangled salt-and-pepper ponytail, he said with a laugh, "I never spoke to an Outlaw before. I'll probably catch a bunch of shit for this."

"Not if they know you were talking to Big Pete from Chicago."

"You're a pretty cool cat. I'm going to tell everyone about you."

"PR from a Hells Angels supporter," Debbie shook her head.

"'*All clubs, all people*,' joined together for a common cause—nondiscrimination," I parroted the party line.

We headed to the elevator to prepare for the Silver Spoke Award Banquet, being held in the grand ballroom. TK joined us, along with three Phantom Lords and two Red Devils, all Hells Angels supporters. TK did not acknowledge me, did not hint at our earlier bond. He/they morphed into what they *were*: rivals.

Debbie's breathing was labored as we waited for the elevator doors to open. She later told me that the hand I laid on her back felt like a brand. We communicated almost telepathically—*Keep calm, no fear, no sudden moves.* We were committed to the outcome. The doors whooshed open and sucked us inside. We hugged the back wall. TK and his supporters stepped behind us, so close their shoulders touched. Weapons flashed on their hips, ankles, and fingers: ball-peen hammers, man-made blades, and silver knuckle-dusters.

Debbie pushed the button for the sixth floor; no one chose a different destination. As the numbers flashed dim yellow—one, two, three—seconds felt like minutes. The elevator doors slid open on four. A petite bride and her five maids dressed in crinkly blue satin stared wide-eyed at us.

Horror registered on their faces; giggles immediately suppressed to coughs. Smiles vanished.

"We'll wait," the bride said as she backed away.

Trapped in a moving grave with six rivals, I contemplated my exit. *No sudden moves.* Debbie's hand grazed the hilt of her knife. In the wall-to-wall mirrors, I pictured blood-smeared panels, a body count, Debbie's long pretty hair sticky and wet, clumps of scalp in my hand. We stopped on the sixth floor. The doors opened.

"See you guys later." Debbie and I stepped out. Blood rushed to my head. TK and his five helpers followed us down the hall.

Shit, what was happening?

Debbie's face blanched. She focused on the mosaic rug. *Keep walking;* I gently pushed her forward. We quickly walked the few paces to our room.

"Do you have your key?" I wanted to keep my hands free *just in case.*

Debbie fumbled for her card, her hands shaking. She dropped it on the ground, scrambled to pick it up, and shoved it into the lock. *Click.* The little green light flashed.

TK and his clan stopped next to us; the hair on the back of my neck pricked. Debbie looked at me, her eyes pleading, *Do we go inside and risk another closed encounter?*

"Well, have a good evening," TK finally broke the silence as he shoved his key into a door and ushered his group inside.

"Holy fuck," we said as we both collapsed on the bed. "What are the odds of *that*? They have the room next door?"

•   •   •

After breakfast the next morning, TK and the others stood wall to wall in a roomful of thousands (all wearing their club colors) and listened to a minigovernment assembly comprised of state senators, a mayor, and several lawyers explain to us bikers the subtle nuances of certain bills, legislation, and strategies for repeal.

"We're all here to protect the lifestyle that comes with wearing the MC patch," a lawyer for the motorcycle company AIM said as he described the latest successful challenges to injustice.

He cited the government's Defender Program, which successfully pressured the prosecution to bring a manslaughter charge against a blind female motorist with no license who'd "killed a biker and received a slap on the hands." She was subsequently sentenced to twelve years in prison, he told us, eliciting resounding applause from our audience.

The lawyer stressed the pitfalls of the Patriot Act (passed shortly after 9/11 and used initially to round up known terrorists and ship them to Guantanamo), an "absolutely unconstitutional" provision that has "outlived its usefulness" and now "gives law enforcement the authority to arrest you and hold you without due process." More cheers from the crowd. But "the worst affront," the lawyer said, practically inciting a riot with this news, "is legislation that threatens to lump motorcycle clubs along with street gangs. . . . The Defender Program has tabled it—it's been tabled." Huge applause.

"Hope we didn't keep you up last night," TK said with

a grin at the break. He was alone and could speak freely. "I told those guys you were Boss of the Outlaws."

"Yeah, okay." I smiled.

"You know"—he lowered his voice—"you should party with us."

Hours later, I settled into the lobby of the hotel in large overstuffed comfy chairs: "Big People Furniture." TK and his entourage walked by. No eye contact; no acknowledgment—again, in "the club zone." Debbie glanced at me.

"Fuck this." I spread my hands on the armrest. "I'm going up."

Alarm registered in Debbie's expression.

"Are you sure?"

"Yes."

"If you're not down in five minutes should I send in a rescue party?"

"Yes."

I knocked on TK's door. I heard a click inside, and what sounded like a loud thud. TK slid back the dead bolt; behind him, Phantom Lords pressed against the wall.

"Want a blast?"

"Yeah, sure." TK ushered me inside. Cocaine lined a flat mirror on the coffee table. I really didn't feel like sitting. The chair was a snack-sized version of the one in the lobby.

"Listen, I want to talk to you."

TK glanced at his roommates. He rubbed his hands on his jeans and nodded toward the balcony. We stepped into the warm night. He slid the Arcadia door shut.

"The Outlaws are headed to Laconia next week. This you-and-me kumbaya shit ends here. In Laconia, if I see you in the halls it's going to be a different story."

"That sucks."

"This is the life we chose. We're rivals."

TK nodded. "How do you want to play this?"

"We stay away from each other."

It was the right call. Several months later I learned TK and his supporters became Hells Angels.

26

THE HELP

You're fucked and you shall remain fucked.

—BIG PETE

Pete and Lou (aka "Bastardo")

"I want to help." Bastardo took a sip of beer.

"Do I look like I need help?"

"Let me probate."

I shook my head.

"Is this because you exiled me once?"

"No."

"I gave up everything for that broad." Bastardo peeled the label off his bottle. "I even left the Black Pistons."

"I know."

"I married her . . . for like five minutes." He laughed.

"That's not why I'm saying no."

"Then why?"

It was late. We were the only ones left in the bar. The place was drafty.

"Because you want to be an Outlaw and there aren't any left."

Bastardo pretended to read the ingredients on the beer label. I could tell he was crushed. He had a vision of the Outlaws the way they *were* in the '90s after the bombings. But thanks to Santa and Ray Rayner and other clowns, the Chicago Outlaws were just a bastardized version of their gangster cousins.

Still, I relented. "If you really want to do this, I'll sponsor you."

"I really want to do this." Bastardo brightened.

We climbed on our bikes, cruised down Mannheim Road, Bastardo looking every bit my reflection, a huge grin on his face. Then his .38 snub-nose slipped out, hit the road hard, and fired off a bullet.

If I had not been drinking, I would have shot him.

• • •

Brothers were eager to offer advice to Bastardo (even though he needed none). "The key," the Outlaw Judas said as he pretended to read an article in the *Chicago Tribune,* "is do not murder anyone"—this tip coming from a felon who'd served six years in prison for "self-defense" after stabbing his victim twenty times in the back.

"What's that word say?" He shoved the article at me. It was upside down.

" 'The,' " I said.

"Why do you got to be such an asshole?"

"He's a terrible enforcer," Coyote remarked once about Judas. "He never finds *anyone.*"

It was true. I'd once wanted to send a cease-and-desist message to a bar owner who lived above his bar, and directed Judas to "deliver it."

Several hours later Judas reported back to me, "I couldn't find him. He's slippery."

"Devils Disciples are trying to start a chapter here." Coyote had tracked down his source and gave Judas the information on him.

"Follow up with that," I ordered. "The guy has no job and sleeps on his mother's couch."

Predictably, Judas returned with nothing. "I couldn't find him."

"Why do you keep him?" Bastardo asked.

"Damage control. If I don't keep him occupied he will become a real problem."

Grease's warning echoed in my head: "There's a *reason*

people got nicknames. That one Judas, he's not young enough to know everything . . . yet."

"The president of Sin City Deciples refuses to accept that you Outlaws sanctioned us." The Professor's voice boomed over *The Jerry Springer Show*. I adjusted the volume on the television. It was still early, at least two hours before I planned to head into the "office."

"First of all," I said, loud and slow, "I never *sanction* anything, and don't ever use that word again." I pictured Feds, like crocodiles, lurking in swampy shallows, just waiting to surface and snap off the heads of small bait for what they called "predicate acts" under RICO. The last thing I needed was for the Outlaws to be "sanctioning" Ma and Pa Kettle" as they trafficked in arms or drugs.

A Sin City Deciple got on the line. "They're saying you *sanctioned* them."

"We're *friends*. Their club supports us."

"We don't want them running around down here."

"Down where?"

"Gary."

"You *do* realize you're talking to an Outlaw?"

"Yes."

"You can't tell *me* what to do." I shot to my feet. "Put The Professor back on the phone."

"Speaking."

"What the fuck is *wrong* with you?"

"Hold up—he wants to talk to you again." The Professor put me on hold.

I threw the remote at Jerry Springer's head and put a small chip in the television.

A few seconds later: "I'm going to have to report this to my National," the voice mumbled over the line.

"Report what?"

"That your club sanctioned Ole Skool Road Playerz."

That word again.

"National will be in touch with you."

"You do whatever the fuck you feel you have to. Goodbye."

Debbie whisked a dozen eggs into a bowl. She arched a brow. "I know that tone."

"What tone?"

"That icy, monosyllabic 'gubye' you reserve for people you plan to hurt."

Two hours later, my cell buzzed. Caller ID flashed a Gary, Indiana, area code.

"Big Pete speaking."

"This is Monster from Sin City." The voice threw me; the caller sounded *white.* Since when did a shine club *sanction* a brother from another race?

"This is a respect thing," Monster continued. "We respect the Outlaws. But we want reciprocation."

"Reciprocation?"

"When you or your supporters ride into Indiana, just give us some notice."

That sounded reasonable enough.

"Glad we have an understanding."

• • •

Two days later, Monster called again. "I've been thinking about our conversation, and I just wanted to tell you that I appreciate the respect. I'm glad we can talk like this—means a lot."

"Everything okay, Boss?" Cockroach said as he poked his head into my office and dipped his hand into my jar of red Licorice Whips.

"Fucking weird call," I said. "Little issue with The Professor and Sin City Deciples."

"What's the problem *now*?" He nibbled the candy vine like an insect.

"Some guy named Monster said he's the head of Sin City, but he spoke like a white guy."

"Monster, the ex–Hells Angel?"

"Are you Monster, the ex-HA?" I asked when I called. I couldn't help it; I was curious.

"No, I'm the Monster from Sin City."

"Were you once a Hells Angel?"

"I was once an Invader too."

Monster, the ex-HA, ex-Invader head of Sin City, invited me to lunch. He chose a quaint bistro in Chicago. When he walked through the door, he blocked the patches of sun on the little square tables.

I tried to make light of his club choices. "Are you having some kind of identity crisis?" His black vest with red lettering barely covered his chest. Embroidered on his right shoulder: "These Colors Don't Shit."

"I like this place—no booths." At six feet eight inches tall, he would never have wedged onto a bench.

His face was a planet. And I realized in that moment, as we shared spaghetti and glazed buttered rolls, that there were few places for freaks like him (like me) to really *belong* and not just *fit*. Here, he had a role, a purpose. He felt needed. Size, color, smarts: None of that mattered. Club politics was about respect and diplomacy.

"So . . . Sin City?"

"I thought I could help them out." Monster tore apart his bun and ate only the crusted edges.

"And they were . . . okay with that?"

He shrugged. "Look at me."

He had a point.

"How long are you going to do this gig?"

"I'm actually thinking about moving west. Maybe I'll become a Vago."*

Pinkie smacked her gum in my ear. "I need a vacation. Florida, Disney World. Do you know anyone there who could show me a good time?"

Besides Mickey Mouse? I made a few calls. "My partner is coming into town—take care of her for me, will you?"

Cockroach, Boss of the South Side, called me a week later. "Brothers from Florida want to meet." I met them in a parking lot, because all "cryptic" conversations deserved to be held outside, out of earshot of listening Feds. Cockroach pressed his oddly shaped torso flat against a car door.

---

* He actually became one. (Vagos and Hells Angels are chief rivals.)

"Why we got to meet out here?" Cockroach asked.

You probably had trouble getting out of the eighth grade, the Feds have a ninety-seven percent conviction rate . . . and their money is encrypted.

"In case the Feds are listening."

He had huge black spots for eyes, long greasy hair, and a few stiff hairs that jutted from his mouth like antennae. Dozer, Boss of the Florida Outlaw chapter, folded his arms across his chest; he was pasty white, with a swastika branded on his arm. A zipper tattoo snaked across his neck. He resembled a pit bull: short, cropped ears and sleek, stocky build. His clan looked chiseled from the same stone, each with the same intense smile found only on the exceptionally dangerous.

"We want to establish a white supremacist presence in Chicago." Dozer leaned forward, baring his big teeth. In my mind's eye, images of The Professor, Preacher Mon, and other shines I had befriended burned on imaginary flaming crosses.

As chairman of the COC, I most definitely was not going to bless discrimination and risk disbanding clubs whose loyalty I'd worked hard to gain. Never mind that in 2000 the club modified its patch to *remove* the swastika because of its overwhelming appeal to white supremacists. Besides, I wasn't into terrorizing people, at least not with hate crimes. I was trying to unite them.

I looked to Cockroach, who suddenly found something fascinating on the floor in front of him.

I covered my mouth when I spoke, paranoid about being videotaped. I didn't want the Feds to lip-read.

"Since our businesses don't conflict, I wish you the best

of luck." Somehow it sounded better when Don Vito Corleone said it in *The Godfather*.

My phone rang at three in the morning. Caller ID flashed Pinkie's number.

"Shit. Shit!" Her voice shook.

"You sound drunk." I propped up on my elbow. Debbie slept soundly next to me.

"The Feds want to talk to me. . . ."

"Did you piss off Donald Duck?"

"Not funny." She sounded like she was about to cry.

Debbie stirred. "Everything okay?"

"Fine, everything's fine." I dismissed Pinkie's call as paranoia—*easy to confuse the Feds for the cops.*

"This is *serious,*" Pinkie spat. "I may have said some things. . . ."

Now I was fully awake. I tossed off the sheets, dropped my legs over the side of the bed.

"What things?"

"I told them about you."

"Told who?"

"The Feds."

"What *about* me?"

"That you were my partner, that you were in tight with the cops up there."

What the fuck was she talking about?

"I was in a lot of pain." She started to cry. "I asked if he had any Vicodin."

"Asked who?"

"Josh."

"Who the fuck is Josh?"

She was sobbing now.

I was on my feet, pacing. There could be only one reason Pinkie called in the wee hours of morning so distraught . . . only one reason the Feds would be interested in someone like Pinkie . . . if *Josh* turned out to be a confidential informant, if she cut a deal. . . .

My mind raced as I recalled a second meeting in a parking lot, a white glazed man with penetrating blue eyes, passing me trinkets—hats, glasses, mugs, all marked with a swastika.

"Is this a game show? What the fuck am I supposed to do with these?" I'd said. I was a smart-ass.

"Everything okay?" Debbie mumbled. *Yeah, sure, everything's fine. Everything's fine.*

"I'm so sorry." I could barely understand Pinkie now. "I had no choice. . . ."

My vision blurred. My head throbbed with the night's activities. *What the fuck was she talking about?* My hair smelled of smoke. My boots still had wet splotches from spilled alcohol.

"Josh was part of the Kavallerie Brigade operation. He helped the Feds infiltrate the white supremacists. The Feds think since you're my partner . . . that you might be involved. . . ."

Involved in what?

"I'm so sorry. . . ." Her voice faded. *This was unbelievable.* I stared at Debbie. Her eyes flicked open.

I knew her; knew her every mood, experienced her every emotion, knew when to approach, when to back off, when to comfort. I knew her well enough to finish her sentences, even her thoughts. I knew everything about her. But what I never realized until now was that Debbie could read me too, that she knew, despite my best efforts to hide it, when I was seriously disturbed, when it was more than just a normal thing, when it was something big, maybe life-altering.

We went for a ride, just the two of us, the way we sometimes did Sunday mornings, each on our bikes, past the bakery on the corner, windburned, the skyline enveloping the city in white gauze. Today was Debbie's birthday. Somehow that seemed impossible, not that she was ever *born*, but that she ever survived another, different life before me, before the Outlaws, before definition and purpose.

Pete and Debbie (EZ Rider rodeo Morris, Illinois)

We stopped at our Dairy Queen, ordered swivel cones from the counter lady with the red lips and teased hair, and slid into our plastic Technicolor booth. We licked our ice creams, not saying much, smiling with our eyes.

I wanted this sort of suspended animation to last. I wanted to be just Pete for a few minutes longer. Busy vanilla people surrounded us; they picked at their French fries and squeezed ketchup on their burgers. They chattered noisily with their kids. Some looked like they'd just arrived from church, garishly overdressed, smelling like incense and burnt hair.

My cone was the size of my hand; I could have swallowed the whole thing in one gulp, but I consciously slowed the pace. No matter how anxious, fatigued, or even agitated I became at life, Debbie was my balm. But the interlude never lasted.

Later that night fists pounded on my front door.

"What's happening?" Debbie froze, her hands foamy with dishwashing soap.

"I'll handle this," I said, but before I could respond, a federal task force stormed in, guns drawn, dressed in full battle gear: Kevlar vests, helmets, plastic shields. One aimed his gun at my bulldog.

"Hey!" If they had shot my dog I was positive I would have shot *them*.

My dog scrambled for cover under the couch. "Look, whatever you have on me I'll go peacefully." I was in gym shorts and a T-shirt.

"We're not here for *you*," The federal task force swarmed Debbie. "We have a warrant for your *wife*."

"Pete!" The pot she scrubbed clattered to the floor.

"My *wife*?"

Debbie visibly paled as a Fed cuffed her soapy hands behind her back.

"What are the charges?"

"Drug possession."

"Drugs?"

Debbie opened her mouth to protest. "Don't you say a fucking word!" I told her.

Pete and Brutus

My heart dropped to the floor as Debbie disappeared into the black van.

"The Feds wanted her held without bail for possession of two Vicodin," the lawyer explained over the phone a few hours later. "But I convinced the judge to set a cash amount at fifty thousand dollars. Your wife's hearing is scheduled in a couple of days in Florida. You'll have to retain a lawyer down there."

My head fogged. This was *Debbie*—college-educated, with two degrees *and a real career*. She was a Normal Person;

she had focus and goals and ambition, an overachiever whose biggest worry in life was acing a final exam she had studied for weeks in advance.

Jail didn't happen to people like Debbie.

"They'll have to prove your wife was in Florida," the lawyer continued.

"Mr. James? There's nothing we can do about it tonight. It's almost midnight. Try to get some sleep."

I stood over my empty bed, my legs heavy, as if water-logged. *How did this happen?* My mind reeled with horror scenarios as Debbie surely connected the dots and figured out how Pinkie fit. "You know he's fucking her," a faceless Fed whispered in the dark. *There would be no coming back from that.* I stared at the ceiling. Images of Caesar, Troy, Henry the VIII played tricks on the walls, all of them de-railed by a broad. Everything I had built, fought hard to maintain and sustain, gone, just like that, in a finger snap, *by a Vicodin-popping broad.*

I paid a Florida lawyer $10,000 to handle the mistaken-identity case and commissioned Bastardo to fly with Debbie as my proxy.

"Get her the fuck out of this." The thought of Debbie pacing a cold cell with concrete urine stains flipped my stom-ach. I dialed Pinkie's number and left her a message: "I will solve this problem and then I will deal with you."

It was not an idle threat. But Pinkie disappeared before I could take action.

The press characterized the arrests of six members (in-cluding my wife) as an "inept government investigation" that "cast too wide a net" hoping to "catch anyone doing anything."

"I hate to sound trite, but it's kind of the Al Capone theory of prosecution," the assistant state's attorney remarked. Only instead of tax evasion, the government levied "heavy-duty drug charges to shut down active members."

"He handed the judge Debbie's driver's license," Bastardo said, filling me in on the details of Debbie's court hearing. "The detective couldn't identity her. All he had to do was look at her license and he would have known he'd made a huge mistake."

"They didn't even have the same eye color," Bastardo relayed. "The confidential informant's broad had blue eyes, jet black hair with purple highlights, and was covered in tattoos." *Pinkie.*

Debbie had green eyes, brown hair, and no tattoos.

The judge dismissed the charges.

27

GAME OVER

The die is cast.

—JULIUS CAESAR

One day it happened, like poison in the system. Extreme fatigue; my body shut down. Lights flickered inside—small bursts of power, then crippling darkness. I pissed blood, cramped, and doubled over with back pain.

"What's wrong with you?" Debbie stood at the bathroom door, barefoot, her painted big toe tapping.

"Hangover."

The toe stopped moving.

Secretly I wished the mass on my kidney was a battle wound. *I could accept that; I could understand that.*

"I have cancer," I told Santa, and spent the morning fielding club crises, preparing run schedules, reviewing agendas, acutely aware of time passing.

"I need you to come to Chicago."

In my mind's eye I saw Santa delayed, stopping first at Dairy Queen for an Oreo Blizzard because he liked them, because blazing heat and humidity made him forget he was supposed to be ruthless, Regional Boss of "a highly organized criminal enterprise with a defined, multilevel chain of command whose entire environment revolved around violence."

"Just until I get better."

Santa cleared his throat. "Okay, but you're still going to run the COC, right?" That was a given; Santa had already betrayed the club's trust by failing to curb Ray Rayner's extortion of its members.

Doctors removed my kidney. Das Jew visited me in the ICU; he was the only Outlaw apart from Bastardo who came to see me. I now thought I knew how Grease must have felt when he was in the hospital recovering from his shooting.

"I made Das Jew wait in the hallway," Debbie said. "He was wailing."

Even in my delirious postoperative state, I knew why "the skinny, bald guy with the sleeved arms" paced the hallway. And it wasn't because he liked me. Das Jew needed me to like him. But when he repeatedly dissolved into sobs in my presence, Debbie told him politely to leave.

And later, as I convalesced at home, Das Jew sent "care packages": Carson's rib specials, two full slabs in a box, complete with containers of coleslaw, potatoes, and brownies. Never mind that I had oxygen tubes shoved up my nose.

Maybe he'd finally realized he needed me, because he tried other gifts too—a 42-inch television and a statue of knives.

I hated that I had to "recover" from major surgery and

was ordered to "take it easy." It wasn't me; Big Pete didn't take anything "easy."

At the next regional meeting, the National Boss, Hillbilly, complained to Santa about the White Region: "According to the rules, an officer cannot maintain his position while on medical."

"You have to appoint successors," Santa said.

"I'll be back in a few months." I assembled Judas and Cockroach, because I could count on their bumbling leadership. Anyone else and I might not have had a position when I returned.

"We'll meet once a week; I'll give you an agenda."

But Cockroach missed the first meeting, and the next and the next. And in time, after multiple doctor visits, follow-up appointments, and mandatory procedures, I realized I *wasn't* coming back, that I couldn't lead from a distance. Cockroach and Judas were like frayed puppets cut loose from their master's block.

"I'm done," I said. "It's over."

Piercing truth hit me—I wasn't getting out of this world alive, or even intact. Propped up on pillows, I was outraged that life continued, that shoppers went on pushing carts inside Wal-Mart, people still went to work, motorists honked horns, cops directed traffic, wrote tickets. The sun still shined. Nothing *stopped*. Nothing changed. Nobody really gave a damn about my cancer, my shattered world.

"It'll never be the same," Nunn said. He was large like me, but with "texture": a pocked face from acne scars, barbed-wire tattoos above his elbows that made his arms look oddly puffy. He had been in the club for just over sixteen years.

"We need an election. What do you think about *me* running for Boss?" Thin red lines cracked across his eyes.

"Run it by Bastardo," I said.

"Hey, Boss," Bastardo gushed. "I *won*! The vote was 8–4."

He broke the news to Santa.

"What's *really* going on?" Santa left his post in Peoria to confront me at my bedside. "Judas says you manipulated the vote."

He looked shorter than I remembered. His white beard tucked into his belt, his boots caked with mud.

"I have no idea what you mean." I pointed to my rumpled sheets, drawn curtains, and bottles of prescription pain medications on the nightstand.

He held an emergency meeting.

"What the fuck is up with Santa?" Bastardo filled me in. "He's taking a poll, asking every member whether you forced them to vote for me."

"Doesn't he realize I could have *appointed* you instead of Judas?"

A week later, Santa reversed Bastardo's election.

"Judas is back in."

"Why?"

"I'm putting him back in."

"But he was voted *out*."

"The election was rigged."

In the muted darkness, I dozed off. Two inmates, chained

together, appeared in a dream, at my window. One stared at me, cocked his head, pretended to listen; the other shut his eyes, but prompted me to answer with a soft clang of chains.

"I'm done," I told Santa.

"Too late. I'm throwing you out."

"I quit."

"You can't quit. I threw you out."

"I'm already out."

And like dominoes, the rest fell: Bastardo, Nunn, Stones; resigned, transferred, left.

On February 9, 2015, before a crowd of two hundred people from thirty-five clubs, I gripped the podium for the last time, inhaled sharply, absorbed the sea of loyal faces jutting from dark coats dusted with snow. They reminded me of bobbing heads. And I was their executioner about to deliver the final startling blow.

I didn't rehearse my exit speech; I don't think I even realized it was going to happen when it did. But maybe all great leaders instinctively know when their rule is over, when it's time to leave the stage, end their own production before the bad reviews hit. I knew what I *wanted* to say—that this outlaw life was all a façade, a game, like *Go*. I knew the rules of play well, the one where "white is at the end of his rope" with "no way to increase his liberties [territories]," and the last one too, the "ko rule, which prevents repetitive capture."

The rule simply states:

THE PREVIOUS BOARD POSITION
CANNOT BE RE-CREATED.

I knew that. And even as I said the words—*"I'm done. It's over"*—guilt tugged at me. I could no longer protect the clubs I'd helped form.

The first cry for help came in at eight o'clock, the night of Twisted Image's anniversary party.

Coyote invited me. Only me.

"No, it's your club, your friends. I'll pass."

"Sure, Boss?" Coyote still called me that.

"Yeah."

Debbie and I spent the night instead observing a Hells Angels party. Now that I was no longer officially Regional Boss I could be a curious observer of weeds sprouting through patches of concrete. We took the car, parked a few blocks from the Angels' party, tucked behind rows of Harleys stacked along the curb.

"What do you see?" Debbie strained to see over my shoulder.

"A crowd."

It was true. A small army formed near the entrance. Angel supporters, clubs I had not seen in droves before. My chest tightened. My fingers tingled. I could no longer feel my toes. Pain shot through me. Debbie put her hand on my knee. I shared my binoculars; a piece of my soul slipped away.

"Chicago's lost."

•   •   •

"Boss." Coyote dissolved into a coughing fit. *This didn't sound good.* I put the phone on speaker.

"What's wrong?"

"Judas jumped me." In the background kids wailed, a female sobbed, and a little voice pleaded, "You're going to be okay, Papa? Right?" An ambulance sawed the night.

Coyote filled in the details. . . .

Twisted Image's anniversary party had just begun; brothers and their kids, wives, and family members were arriving. Burgers sizzled on the backyard grill, pitchers of iced lemonade shared space with cases of cold beer. The fence surrounding the clubhouse had a few holes; rusted barbed wire poked through worn grassy sections. Tunnels large enough for rodents popped into the street. The front door burst open; Judas and his entourage of fifteen Outlaws marched inside.

"Sorry we're late, but we missed the invite." Judas flicked his lighter on and off, flames licking the edges of tablecloths. He held it close to Coyote's lips, singed off a few mustache hairs.

"We'll take the rag."

But Coyote resisted; his patch represented everything he believed in: club, code, God, country. "I told him to fuck off."

Judas and several others closed in, circled him like prey, and pounced. Taking hard slams to the jaw, Coyote dropped to his knees. The bottle Coyote gripped shattered and bits of brown glass embedded in his little girl's cheek.

This part of Coyote's story sent chills down my spine. It wasn't wrong for Judas and his Outlaws to attack Coyote;

in fact, if they chose to beat Coyote up every day of the fucking week I wouldn't care. But Judas and the others crossed an invisible line. They acted like thugs, not gangsters. And they exacted retribution in front of wives and children, in front of Coyote's daughter. I was actually amazed Coyote didn't leave in an ambulance.

"He kicked me in the head until my eyes swelled shut. Then he ordered them all to attack. Body after body slammed on top of me, crushed my lungs, flattened my arms to the floor, and shattered my kneecap. I couldn't breathe."

His daughter screamed, *"Papa, Papa, you're going to be all right?"*

"I don't know anymore. Everything's changed."

I let him go. Nausea roared in the back of my throat. I fell into my chair, remote in hand, and stared silently at a blank television screen. My skin itched, as if burned to the pink. It hurt to touch, to cover, to feel anything, even air. This kind of exposure reduced me, shamed me. I was not a part of Judas's Outlaws, *his* gang of marauding psychopaths.

I could no longer protect Coyote or any of the clubs I had helped create. Coyote, like his kids, like *all* of them, begged for deliverance, for relief. They were lambs being brought to the slaughter. And if I closed my eyes, I could see them in the dark, in the stillness, waiting, waiting, as one by one their little necks cracked.

PS

two years later
I could act in a Shakespearean play. But I could not pretend to live.

Cancer spreads. It begins with changes in a single cell or small group of cells. At first the shifts are subtle, barely noticeable. Small discomfort in the core, then sharp bursts of pain signal the first alarms. Fatigue follows, an extreme, debilitating slowdown. Inside, malignant tumors invade nearby tissues, break off, travel through the blood, and form new mutations. My kidneys malfunction. *It's like I'm rotting from the inside.*

When I ask my oncologist about treatment and possible cures, he responds, "There's always hope." *That's not what I asked, and I'm not a "hope" guy.* My games are *Go, Risk, chess, Monopoly,* and building whole civilizations in my mind.

"I don't like these odds," I say. *"Let's start over. You go first."*

He listened, but what could he do? He had already removed one of my kidneys.

Remission is like regrouping, pep-talking the remaining combat soldiers to perform double-time for the same pay. At first they do it willingly. They respect their general. They believe in the mission—the elimination of waste. A rotting foundation will only kill them all. And so they fight, they train, they prepare daily for the rigors of conquest. They survive, but they hardly thrive.

"How are you feeling?" my doctors ask during checkups. I have so many. They test my blood, my urine. They look inside me, but they do not see me.

I have dreams of being an inflatable.

"I'm fine." It's only a partial lie.

It's early March, still frigid cold outside. As I pull into the hospital parking lot for yet another scope, the windchill reminds me of the corn beef and cabbage parties North Side hosted. Every year we celebrated James Earl Ray's birthday. *I know what you're thinking*: He assassinated Martin Luther King; he's a murderer.

I insisted toward the end that we change the theme to St. Patrick's Day. My hypocrisy will only go so far. . . . after all, I chaired a confederation of thirty-seven clubs, some of which had shines as bosses. I fought *against* discrimination and white supremacist factions. My legacy was inclusion (as long as the clubs supported *my* club). No rogues. No malignant cells.

Outlaws circled the North Side clubhouse, cold, anxious.

"Do you think they're ready?" Debbie, who sat in the backseat, wiped frost from the window with her glove. *Sol-*

St. Patrick's Day Party (formerly Corn Beef)

diers are never prepared for the recoil. Still, I liked to give them practice.

"Watch this," and like a switch I flicked on "Angry Pete." I warned Bastardo, "Don't react. I have to get into character and pretend I'm pissed." I slammed the car door, tensed, my hands balled into fists.

I boomed, "What the *fuck* is happening here?"

Brothers scrambled, some falling and nearly toppling to the pavement. Others just stared at me, mouths startled open, completely at a loss as to what to say, do, undo. Wind tickled my beard, cut into my cheeks. I raged on, my voice hollow in my ears as if I were standing at one end of a long tunnel. The brothers lined up single file, heads bowed in supplication, looking ill.

"Everything's ready for you, Boss," one mumbled. *I*

already knew that. Otherwise they would still all be inside the clubhouse.

I played on, enjoying the conflicting emotions my fake tirade caused. "Ready for me? You motherfuckers think you know what I want? You think you know me? You don't know me. You know what I let you know about me."

"There's a dark mass on my other kidney?"

"It's not growing at the moment." The doctor probably thought he was being positive.

"At the moment"? What did that mean?

"Can it be *stopped*?"

"We have to watch it."

It was like watching a dark storm swirling a few miles away. Soon, it would blow in and take with it my soul. It was the most helpless I have ever felt in my life. This wasn't *me* in any form. I didn't *watch* impending chaos voluntarily. I ran the third-largest city in the United States. I spoke regularly to crowds of bikers about topics that mattered. I rallied support for the Chicago Outlaws from clubs who ordinarily despised us. I lived life on my terms. But even Caesar can't be Caesar forever.

I did not *cause* my cancer. Nor can I *stop* the spread of tumors. I can only control the symptoms and make strategic choices that might *slow* the growth. Eventually, I know, I will lose this battle. It's inevitable. Cancer kills. Cancer destroys. Cancer transforms before it rebuilds and multiplies and mutates healthy cells.

The Chicago Outlaws I led are not the Outlaws I left, not the Outlaws who remain.

ACKNOWLEDGMENTS

FROM BIG PETE,

This book has been a labor of love, trust, and faith. It would not have been possible without the help of the following people: Lou "Bastardo" Caracci, the best brother a man could have; as Wyatt Earp said to Doc Holliday, "Thanks for always being there." Maria Palermo, who pitched in whenever asked. Dr. Chadi Nabhan, my oncologist, without whose care I'm not sure I would have survived to write this book.

And these people, who stuck by my side and when things changed never wavered from our friendship: Tony "Kickback" Wallenberg, Scot "Gypse" Patterson, AJ "Mule" Watson, Dave "Redwood" Russell, Thomas "Monster" Williford, Eric "Big Man" Guajardo, Nick and Anna Urso, and my old college buddies John Bourne and Jim Schuessler.

All the men and women of the Confederation of Clubs who didn't abandon me and had the faith to realize I hadn't changed. Thanks, and I love you all.

Next, I would like to give a special loving "Thank you" to my mother, Diana James, and to my father, Ernest P. James, who taught me to be the man I am. I wish you were here so I could tell you I finally made it. To my sister, Demetra Ness, who has shown me so much love. To my late brother, Michael E. James. To my daughter, Jessica, whom I love very much. To my mother- and father-in-law, Dianne and David Plowman, who never judge me. To Luke Plowman, my brother-in-law. To my cousins Demetra, Niko, and Maria Lakerdas. To the Peter and Tana Ladas family who always had a helping hand for me.

I offer a very special thanks to Kerrie Droban, who listened to my tirades and rambling, whose understanding made this book possible. I couldn't have done this with anyone but her. She wrote this book and has become a valued friend. To Bob Diforio, my agent, who did a great job and took my obnoxious questions in stride!

To Brutus James, the best dog a man could ever want, who came into my life at just the right time.

Lastly, I would like to thank my ever-loving wife, Debbie, who has gone above and beyond anything a man could expect from a wife and best friend. Through good times and bad, highs and lows, thick and thin, she has been by my side, my rock. Thank you, my love—you've made me a better man. I love you very much.

Thanks again to all the people I mentioned, and thanks to all the people I've met on this great journey I call my life!!

—Peter "Big Pete" James